THE 100-PAGE SUBSCRIPTION PRICING BOOK

THE 100-PAGE
Subscription
Pricing Book

A SHORT GUIDE TO
Mastering SaaS and XaaS Pricing

FELIX MÖRÉE

HOUNDSTOOTH
PRESS

THE 100-PAGE SUBSCRIPTION PRICING BOOK
A Short Guide to Mastering SaaS and XaaS Pricing

FIRST EDITION

ISBN   978-1-5445-5007-7   *Hardcover*
        978-1-5445-5006-0   *Paperback*
        978-1-5445-5008-4   *Ebook*

Contents

Introduction

PRICING—LOW ATTENTION, BUT HIGH POTENTIAL

Pricing is one of the most overlooked yet impactful areas of business strategy. A study by *SaaS Mag* found that the average SaaS executive, for companies with between 5 to 100 million USD revenue, spends just 11.5 hours over the lifetime of their business defining, testing, and adjusting their pricing.[1] This is surprising given that pricing directly influences annual recurring revenue (ARR) and profitability, critical drivers of success for any subscription business. Despite its importance, pricing often remains an afterthought in many organizations.

However, given its potential, executives should spend more time on pricing. Redesigning pricing can deliver a 10–20 percent increase in ARR with minimal churn,[2] and sometimes even greater gains depending on the product life cycle stage, product stickiness, etc. Beyond recurring revenue, pricing affects key performance indicators (KPIs), such as net retention rate (NRR), gross retention rate (GRR), customer acquisition cost (CAC), conversion rates, and customer lifetime value (CLTV)—all of which are crucial to enterprise value.

So, why does pricing receive so little attention? Several factors contribute:

- **Focus on growth over pricing:** Founders often prioritize user acquisition and adoption, viewing pricing as a barrier rather than a growth lever, with a "grow now, optimize later" mindset.
- **Lack of ownership:** Pricing spans multiple departments—product, sales,

finance, and marketing—leading to a lack of clear accountability and optimization.

- **Limited early data:** Early-stage companies often lack sufficient data to inform pricing, resulting in a "set it and forget it" approach that neglects later adjustments.
- **Perceived complexity:** Pricing requires a deep understanding of customer behavior, market dynamics, and customer's willingness to pay, which many organizations find daunting.
- **Dynamic and evolving nature of pricing:** Shifting customer preferences, willingness to pay, and competition require ongoing adjustments, but many organizations lack the tools or expertise to stay agile.
- **Lack of pricing expertise:** Many companies lack the knowledge/capabilities to develop effective pricing strategies, relying on guesswork, competitor benchmarking, or oversimplified models that fail to capture true value.

Additionally, internal resistance often complicates pricing decisions. The sales teams may oppose pricing adjustments over fear of losing deals, the product team may oppose them due to uncertainty on how to technically implement the changes, and the finance team may hesitate to experiment with pricing due to risk. These challenges make it even harder to prioritize pricing as a strategic tool.

This book aims to make pricing more accessible by providing a short and concise guide on how to work with pricing, from strategy and design to implementation and governance. Whether you're launching a new product or refining an existing strategy, the insights here will help you unlock pricing as a powerful driver of growth and profitability. Due to the format, the book should take slightly more than two hours to read,[3] leaving more than nine hours for implementation to "fill the quota" of 11.5 hours—although you should invest more time in pricing.

GROWTH OF SUBSCRIPTIONS

Subscriptions as a business model have existed for centuries, with early examples like magazine and newspaper subscriptions in the seventeenth century.[4] However, the modern form has evolved significantly with digital technology. The rise of SaaS (Software as a Service) and XaaS (Anything as a Service, e.g., Hardware and Infrastructure as a Service) reflect a more recent shift, driven by cloud computing and widespread internet access.

In the late 1990s and early 2000s, businesses largely relied on on-premises software and infrastructure, which required substantial upfront investments in hardware, licenses, and IT support.[5] This created sales friction and limited ongoing product development, as revenue depended on one-time purchases.

Subscription models addressed these limitations by shifting costs from capital expenditures (CapEx) to operational expenses (OpEx). This made solutions more financially accessible, expanded the potential market, and streamlined purchasing. Lower upfront costs also allowed decisions to be made lower in the organization, speeding up sales cycles.

As internet infrastructure improved, delivering software over the web became viable, leading to the SaaS era. By the mid-2000s, companies like Salesforce pioneered online customer relationship management (CRM) solutions. SaaS enabled recurring revenue to fund continuous innovation, while customers benefited from automatic updates, lower setup costs, and no need for an on-premises infrastructure.

The model has since enabled more stable, long-term product investments while offering customers predictable, low recurring fees. SaaS now spans everything from office tools to project management, becoming a cornerstone of modern business operations and allowing companies to focus more on their core mission.

XaaS expanded on this model by offering broader, cloud-based services beyond software, such as Hardware as a Service (Haas) (e.g., Samsara's IoT devices for fleet management) and Infrastructure as a Service (e.g., the cloud-computing platform Amazon Web Services). These allow organizations to access resources on demand, avoid large capital costs, and pay only for what they use. Growth in XaaS has been supported by affordable sensors enabling accurate usage tracking, and by businesses' need for agility, faster innovation, and rapid adaptation across industries from healthcare to finance.

Adoption of SaaS and XaaS surged in the 2010s as demand grew for cost-effective, scalable, and accessible solutions. The ability to scale on demand and shift to subscription pricing made cloud services an attractive alternative to traditional models. Today, SaaS and XaaS are central to business operations, and subscriptions are increasingly becoming the norm.[6]

SUCCESSFUL PRICING: MOVE FROM A "PROFIT SQUARE" TO A "PROFIT TRIANGLE"

Before digging into the pricing design, it is helpful to understand what defines successful pricing. One fundamental rule for pricing is to understand and capture customers' perceived value. However, your customers' needs and their willingness to pay differ, something your monetization model should account for. The theory for offering differentiation is to move from a "profit square" to a "profit triangle," as you can see in Figure I.1.

For simplicity, let's say you have a unit cost of one hundred and a linear demand curve, as you can see in the figure (see calculations in the footnotes[7]). If you offer only one product at the price of three hundred, you would sell a volume of two thousand units, leading to a profit of four hundred thousand (the dark gray area in the left-hand side of Figure I.1.).[8] But the challenge with having one offering is you miss both the opportunity to sell to customers with lower willingness to pay and to capitalize on customers with a higher willingness to pay, meaning you are not tapping the potential in the light gray area in the figure.

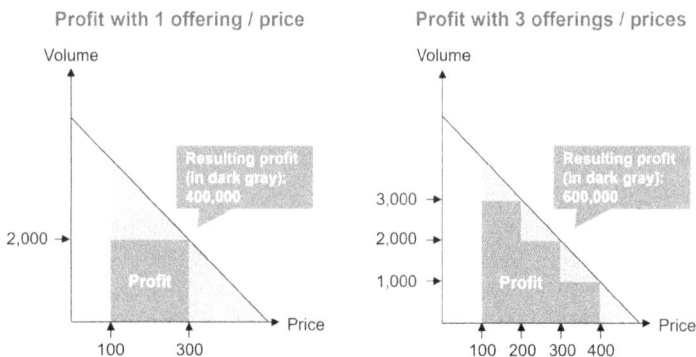

Figure I.1. Profit (in dark gray) with one versus three offerings/prices.

With three offerings, such as a good-better-best model, you could capture the willingness to pay of customers with different needs. For instance, offering products at two hundred, three hundred, and four hundred would increase the profit to six hundred thousand (the dark gray area in the right-hand side of Figure I.1.), a 50 percent improvement compared to a single price point.[9]

Further adjustments, such as introducing more offerings and strategically differentiating price points, can help you capture the full triangle (i.e., capturing also the light gray area in Figure I.1.). In this example, capturing the entire "profit triangle" could raise profits to eight hundred thousand,[10] a 100 percent increase over the single-price approach.

To succeed in achieving a "profit triangle," you need to have differentiated pricing. There are certain considerations for differentiation:

- Customer segmentation: Who to target and how do their needs vary?
- Offering model/packaging: Based on customer needs, what offering do they look for?
- Price model: What factors reflect the value in the product (e.g., number of users, survey responses, leads converted), and how does value scale with the number of units?
- Price level: What is the willingness to pay? How does it vary between customers?
- Price communication: How to sell based on value to different segments?

There is a risk that customers with high willingness to pay could select and pay for an offering targeting customers with low willingness to pay. For example, customers willing to pay four hundred for the product in Figure I.1 may pay only two hundred. Another example is that customers actively or by coincidence use more than what they pay for, such as multiple users sharing one login. Therefore, it is useful to think about "fencing," which are limitations or rules to ensure customers select and pay for what they need and use. Fencing could be achieved in the offering design, where different features are included in different packages, in the price model (e.g., limits of number of users, logins, invoices, etc.), or customer segmentation (e.g., certain packages or prices are offered only to specific customers) that make it possible to steer customers to the right packages and prices.

GENERAL PRICING ADVICE

To set the scene, some general, but helpful, advice on pricing is listed below. These are more overarching concepts to keep in mind when working with pricing:

- **Test willingness to pay early in the product-market fit:**[11] Just because there is a need doesn't mean there is a willingness to pay. Ask questions about price levels to understand if your product can be sold at a price larger than zero.
- **Think price equals value:** Prices should be set based on value. A rule of thumb could be to think that if it generates value, you should probably charge for it.
- **Measure perceived value:** It's the perceived value that matters when setting a price, which should consider both hard and soft benefits. For example, hard benefits include savings and increased revenue, while soft benefits include your brand, reputation, and customer interactions.

- **Go beyond the price point:** Pricing is more than a price point. Successful pricing is more about the architecture and the process, rather than the price itself. What you charge for and how you charge often trump how much you charge.
- **Differentiate more:** Your customers are different; therefore, you must ensure your offering also caters to different needs.
- **Be transparent but not comparable:** Ideal pricing should be transparent to customers in regard to what value they receive and what they pay for, but it should be difficult to make a direct comparison with competitors.
- **Find the sweet spot:** Customers will say, "You are too expensive" because they always want lower prices. There is a difference between being expensive and being so expensive that customers leave.
- **Pilot significant changes:** Update and refine your pricing continuously to meet changes in customer needs and their willingness to pay. Test larger changes on selected deals or segments before implementing a change on all customers to ensure it brings the desired outcomes.

These guidelines can provide initial direction in your pricing journey and will be explored further in the coming chapters. However, ensure that you have a working product and the necessary internal processes (e.g., onboarding) as well. Pricing can improve many KPIs, but it can't fix technical and operational issues—those need to be identified and addressed separately.

TARGET AUDIENCE AND THE STRUCTURE OF THIS BOOK

This book aims to provide a high-level understanding of the key elements and steps for successful pricing of new or existing subscriptions. Due to the length, it is not possible to go in-depth on all topics, but there are references to sources covering those topics.

The target audience is companies that offer subscriptions with some product-market fit,[12] including a decent understanding of the company's ideal customer profile (ICP). There is a wide range of material on finding product-market fit,[13] so the book will not cover that in much detail. In addition, it is assumed that some initial work on market prioritization and potential estimation has been done, and these topics are also not a focus of this book. The target roles in those organizations are everyone working with or interested in pricing.

The book is split into three themes with two to three subchapters each, shown in Figure I.2. The first theme is about the underlying strategy. Thoughtful packaging and pricing are based on the overall strategy of a company, an understanding of customer segments, and a plan for which channels to use. Next, the main building blocks of the packaging and pricing are discussed, i.e., what to charge for, how to charge, and how much to charge. Last, when the packaging and pricing are designed, there are chapters on topics that are important in the execution/practical usage of the new monetization model: how to sell, monitor, and update it continuously. Each of the following chapters concludes with a summary to help reinforce the key takeaways and make them easier to reference later.

The book is generally written in a context of business-to-business (B2B) SaaS. To highlight differences for managed services, service contracts, HaaS, two-sided markets, business-to-consumer (B2C) settings, and offerings with significant onboarding, there is a special chapter at the end of the book. Generally, the pricing differences between SaaS and XaaS, as well as between B2B and B2C, are not as large as one may believe.

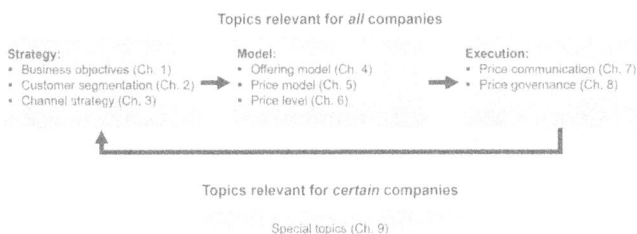

Figure I.2. The structure of this book.

Although the process may seem quite linear, it is important not to see the pricing process as a waterfall process. Rather, you should view it as a loop that should continuously be refined. When working with your pricing, be prepared to occasionally go back one or multiple steps to refine or revise a previous step.

The final chapter offers a condensed summary of the entire book, outlining the key steps involved in a packaging and pricing redesign for easy future reference. At the end of the book, you'll also find a glossary summarizing all acronyms.

CASE STUDY

Throughout this book, but particularly in Chapters 4 and 5, you will find examples that many readers can relate to: an AP (accounts payable) automation product. This example provides consistency and context, supplemented by other specific examples per chapter. Here's a brief introduction to what such a solution entails.

AP automation solutions enable buying organizations to receive invoices, manage approvals, and process payments automatically through a single platform.[14] Typically, these solutions include several key components:

- **Capture and archive:** Collect and store invoice data from both digital and physical invoices, maintaining a clear audit trail of all actions.
- **Matching and workflow:** Match invoices to purchase orders (POs) and goods receipts, or route them automatically to the relevant team or individual for review and approval.
- **Approval automation:** Streamline recurring invoices and approval workflows using, e.g., AI-driven processes for enhanced accuracy and efficiency.
- **Analytics and benchmarking:** Analyze invoice data and compare AP performance metrics against industry standards to drive process improvements.

This example will serve as a practical reference point throughout the book, helping to illustrate key concepts related to offering models, price models, and price levels.

CHAPTER 1

Business Objectives

KEY COMMERCIAL GOALS

As a first step in the pricing journey, determine what your overarching goals are for your pricing. These should be influenced by the overall strategy and goals that are ultimately set by the company owners. This book will not dig deep into all possible strategies, but rather it will focus on a few key goals and trade-offs to consider.

In particular, a key decision is to determine if the most important goal is ARR growth or profitability. Depending on where you want to focus the most, you typically have these three cases:

- **Full focus on ARR growth:** In this situation, a company typically wants to penetrate a market and/or increase market share. Prioritize customer acquisition with competitive pricing to attract new customers or win them from competitors. The focus is on winning customers at almost any cost, leading to aggressive pricing across the board to win customers. Just be mindful not to trigger a price war.
- **Full focus on profitability:** Here, acquiring new customers is not the most important, or at least not to acquire them at any cost by using, for example, a skimming approach. Instead, the focus is on deepening relationships with existing customers through upselling and cross-selling. Boost monetization with add-ons and additional services while retaining customers.
- **Balanced focus on ARR growth and profitability:** In this situation, you prioritize both to a certain extent. Use a "land and expand" strategy with

low-cost starting offerings and clear upsell paths. Where the starting offering can be discounted aggressively to win new customers, while there is a strategy for increasing prices and upselling new features further on to increase profitability.

The priorities may shift over time. A new product or feature might start with full focus on ARR growth before the focus shifts to maximizing profit. This has been seen among companies such as the music-streaming service Spotify, where focus has shifted from growth to profitability, which became evident when Spotify's CEO referred to 2024 as "the year of monetization."[15] To achieve that, price adjustments were a key lever.

The trade-off between growth and profitability has been formalized in the "Rule of 40," which has been a popular method to assess SaaS companies' performance.[16] The rule implies that the sum of ARR growth in percentage and the profit margin (often EBITDA) in percentage should be larger than forty, showing that a company should either grow very rapidly or be very profitable. Note that it doesn't have to be black and white. It's possible to go for a strategy in between as well that balances ARR growth and profitability to a different extent.

STRATEGIC TRADE-OFFS

Besides profitability versus ARR growth, you should consider several other strategic trade-offs when designing a new packaging and pricing strategy. Keep in mind you don't have to choose one of the extremes. You can balance the two as well and "do both" to different extents. But the two extremes present the trade-offs you need to consider.

One key trade-off in pricing is between monetization and the cost of sales. Charging customers exactly what they need and are willing to pay requires a highly flexible offering and substantial marketing and sales resources, making it challenging in practice. At the other extreme, a simple offering with fewer options may shorten the sales process but often results in excessive discounting and lost revenue. The goal is to balance incremental monetization with manageable sales costs.

Positioning the company as a premium provider or a value-priced provider is another trade-off. Premium providers deliver high-quality features and exceptional support, justifying higher prices and fostering loyalty, but often limiting customer reach. In contrast, value providers focus on affordability and simplicity, appealing to cost-conscious users but requiring operational efficiency to sustain margins.

Another trade-off is focusing on niche customer segments versus targeting a mass market. Niche strategies tailor offerings to specific industries, enhancing loyalty and reducing competition, but limiting scalability. Mass-market approaches attract broader audiences, increasing revenue potential but risking brand dilution and tougher competition from established players. Additionally, companies must decide whether to lead on pricing or follow competitors. Price leaders set market trends and enhance brand authority, but risk customer pushback if pricing is misaligned with market readiness. Price followers minimize risk by aligning with competitors but often sacrifice profit margins and differentiation.

Finally, businesses must choose whether they should focus on acquiring new customers or deepening relationships with existing ones. New customer acquisition grows the user base but is resource-intensive with a longer path to profitability. Without any retention measures, the customer base bleeds out. Focusing on retention and upselling existing customers is more cost-effective but requires that the offering portfolio is broad enough, and can limit growth potential while increasing vulnerability if retention declines. However, without acquiring any new customers, the upselling to existing customers will be saturated.

To give some examples, consider the construction management software Procore and the communications platform Zoom that appear to represent contrasting strategies across key trade-offs.[17] Procore takes a niche, premium approach, targeting the construction industry with tailored features, deep integrations, and high-touch service. Its offering is more complex and involves a longer sales process, resulting in higher acquisition costs, but it enables strong monetization through expansion within accounts. As a price leader, Procore justifies higher prices with specialized value and industry expertise, focusing more on upselling and retaining existing customers as they grow.

Zoom, by contrast, follows a mass-market, value-driven strategy with simple pricing, self-service onboarding, and broad appeal. Its standardized offering supports rapid scaling at a low sales cost. Zoom has largely followed market pricing to stay competitive and accessible, fueling growth through fast customer acquisition before introducing upsell paths like Zoom Phone. While Zoom prioritizes simplicity and reach, Procore emphasizes depth and specialization, highlighting the different strategic paths companies can take.

·

MONETIZATION MODEL TRADE-OFFS

In addition to the strategic trade-offs, several model design trade-offs must be considered as well. As with the strategic trade-offs previously, you don't have to focus on one or another. You can very well split your focus between the two extremes.

One key consideration is choosing between different price metrics for various products (e.g., number of users for one product and number of documents for another product) or a single metric for all (e.g., number of users for all products). Using different metrics tailors pricing to a product's unique value, enhancing customer satisfaction but adding complexity and potential confusion. A single metric simplifies pricing and management but risks overlooking individual product value, possibly leaving revenue untapped.

Another balance to strike is between simple and complex monetization models. Simple models with straightforward subscription plans are easy for the sales team to explain and for customers to understand, which speeds up decisions. However, simplicity may limit revenue by failing to address varied customer needs. Complex models with multiple tiers and add-ons capture more value by catering to diverse needs, but risk being complicated to sell while also overwhelming customers, causing confusion and longer sales cycles.

Pricing approaches also differ between competitive/cost-based and value-based pricing. Competitive pricing aligns with market rates or production costs, minimizing risk but potentially undervaluing unique features. Value-based pricing maximizes revenue by reflecting customers' perceived value but requires deeper insights into customer needs and market dynamics, making it more resource-intensive.

Additionally, businesses must decide on client-level targeted pricing versus a single price level for all. Targeted pricing enhances relevance and competitiveness but complicates structures, while a single price offers simplicity but may miss capturing varying customer value.

Last, consider whether you should communicate one total price or break down individual components priced separately. Presenting one total price simplifies the buying process but may obscure feature value. Breaking down components highlights value but risks overwhelming buyers with excessive detail and risks starting discussions with your customers that you would want to avoid, such as negotiating specific items when you sell bundles.

Examples of these trade-offs can be found for Google and Salesforce.[18] Google focuses on simplicity and scalability. For example, Google Workspace uses straightforward tiered packaging with few add-ons, making it easy for customers to understand and adopt quickly. Its pricing aligns with competitive benchmarks, ensuring broad appeal but potentially missing out on capturing additional value from high-usage customers.

Salesforce, on the other hand, emphasizes flexibility and value capture. It offers complex packaging with multiple tiers, add-ons, and customization options tailored to specific industries and use cases. This approach maximizes revenue by addressing diverse customer needs but requires a more complex sales process and higher management resources.

Navigating these trade-offs is crucial for designing effective packaging and pricing strategies, as they represent fundamental considerations in your overall design. While this chapter introduces the key concepts, you may need to revisit and refine your strategy as you explore the upcoming chapters on customer segmentation and channel strategy. These additional insights will help ensure your pricing aligns with customer needs, market conditions, and business objectives.

DETERMINE WHERE TO BE ON THE TRADE-OFFS

Each trade-off described in this chapter represents a spectrum of choices, like growth vs. profitability or simplicity vs. precision in pricing. The goal isn't necessarily to choose extremes but to understand where your company should sit on each dimension. There's no one-size-fits-all answer—what's right depends on your goals, market, and capabilities. Use the following factors as a guide:

- **Company strategy and owner objectives:** Align pricing with whether you're optimizing for ARR growth, profitability, a combination of the two, or something else.
- **Product maturity and market position:** Early-stage offerings may benefit from adoption-focused pricing, while mature products can prioritize monetization.
- **Customer behavior and willingness to pay:** Use research and feedback to understand factors like niche segments to target, the acceptable complexity of your price model, acceptable price variations, and how best to communicate pricing.
- **Internal capabilities:** Ensure your organization can support the complexity of your packaging and pricing, especially for sales, marketing, and billing systems.
- **Competitive landscape and industry benchmark:** Study how others price similar offerings to decide where to align or differentiate.

By systematically evaluating these factors, you'll be better equipped to select a pricing strategy that fits your broader commercial goals and to evolve it as needed. Pricing is not a one-time decision. It's a strategic lever that should adapt alongside your product, customers, and market conditions.

Also, reflect on your leadership team's risk tolerance. How aggressively are you willing to experiment or push pricing boundaries? Consider your need for long-term flexibility as well, and then choose an approach that can scale and evolve as your offering and customer base grow.

Finally, pilot and iterate. Test new pricing strategies on smaller customer segments to validate their impact before initiating a broader rollout. Learning early reduces risk and helps you fine-tune your packaging and pricing.

GET EVERYONE ONBOARD

To set a strategy and to get everyone to follow it are two different things. A helpful exercise is to ask people in the organization to rate where the company should be on some trade-offs. The results are then compared with what management states. Normally, you get an outcome as in Figure 1.1, where different functions have different views on where the company should be. For example, management may prioritize profitability to ensure long-term sustainability, while the sales team may focus on maximizing growth to hit short-term sales targets or earn commissions. This misalignment can lead to conflicting actions. For instance, management pushes for higher pricing to improve margins, while the sales team heavily discounts to close deals quickly. Based on the results from the exercise, focused discussions (and/or incentive adjustments) may be required within the organization to get alignment on those trade-offs where there are differences in views.

Outcome from internal exercise regarding goal trade-offs for a company
All the way to the left means 100% focus on the left statement, and all the way to the right means 100% of the focus should be on the right statement.

Maximize ARR growth	Maximize profitability
Be a premium provider	Be a value-priced provider
Target niche customer segments	Target mass market
Be a price leader	Follow competitors' prices
Acquire new customers	Deepen relations with existing customers

Alignment needed to ensure everyone is working toward the same goal

Respondents: Management   Marketing   Sales   Product

Figure 1.1. Results from an internal goal trade-off exercise. Responses are aggregated per function.

SUMMARY

- **Set overall goals for the commercial operations:** Companies must decide whether to prioritize ARR growth, profitability, or a balance of both, shaping their pricing and sales strategies accordingly.
- **Determine key trade-offs (e.g., growth vs. profitability):** Businesses face several trade-offs, e.g., monetization vs. cost of sales, premium vs. value positioning, niche vs. mass market, and pricing leadership vs. following competitors. Decide where you want to be to inform your pricing.
- **Get everyone aligned on the strategy:** Misalignment between management and teams (e.g., sales focusing on winning every deal at any price while leadership prioritizes profitability) can lead to conflicting actions. Conducting internal alignment exercises helps unify strategic direction and optimize execution.

CHAPTER 2

Customer Segmentation

THE CASE FOR A NEED-BASED SEGMENTATION

Trying to sell to everyone is inefficient and costly. Segmentation helps you prioritize by identifying which customer groups to focus on—and just as importantly, which ones *not* to. It enables your team to tailor offerings, messages, and pricing strategies to better meet specific customer needs and increase your commercial impact.

Many companies begin with an ICP—a description of the type of customer most likely to benefit from their product, often based on factors like industry, size, or geography. While ICPs are useful, they can be misleading if built solely on demographic characteristics. A classic example, shown in Figure 2.1, illustrates this well: two individuals with the same gender, birth year, country of origin, marital status, and housing situation might appear identical in a demographic segmentation.[19] Yet if one is the king of England and the other is rock star Ozzy Osbourne, it's clear they have dramatically different needs.

This highlights a key flaw: segmenting based on who customers *are* doesn't always tell you *what they need*. A stronger approach is to start by identifying what drives demand for your product and then use demographics to find customers with those needs. That requires a clear understanding of how your product is used in practice. For example, we worked with a data analytics company that charged per user. Some clients used the tool daily as a core part of their external consulting services, while others accessed it only occasionally for internal reporting. The same price metric applied to both, yet the value they received—and their willingness to pay—varied significantly.

	Person A	Person B
Gender	Male	Male
Birth year	1948	1948
Born in	England	England
Marital status	Married	Married
Housing	Castle	Castle

Figure 2.1. Two individuals who are similar in a demographic segmentation.

Needs-based segmentation also helps uncover pricing potential. Take water: tap water is nearly free, while bottled water can cost several dollars. Though the core product is the same, factors like convenience, context, branding, and occasion dramatically shift perceived value. The same is true for your product. One company might see it as a compliance necessity, another as a productivity driver, and a third as a nice-to-have, each with different urgency and price sensitivity.

In short, segmenting by needs rather than appearance leads to smarter targeting, more tailored pricing, and better business outcomes.

CHARACTERISTICS OF A GOOD SEGMENTATION

A good segmentation breaks your market into distinct groups that your teams, such as sales, marketing, or customer success, can treat differently in a meaningful way. "Treating differently" might involve using different marketing messages, tailoring offers and prices, or emphasizing specific sales arguments. In pricing, it can help you determine what to include in packages, set price levels, and improve sales conversion.

A useful way to assess the quality of your segmentation is through the acronym BADAS(S):

- **Believable:** The segmentation dimensions make intuitive sense and are logical.
- **Actionable:** The segmentation allows for practical application, such as tailoring communications and strategies by segment.
- **Differentiable:** There are clear differences between the segments, with members being similar within each group but distinct from other groups in the variables that matter.
- **Accessible:** The segments can be effectively reached and served in practice.

- **Substantial:** Segments are large enough to justify attention and resource allocation.

It's not uncommon to use multiple segmentations across the customer journey. For example, one segmentation might guide brand positioning and marketing, while another supports acquisition and onboarding, and a third helps optimize pricing or retention strategies. The key is that each segmentation must be practical and relevant for its intended use.

In terms of the number of segments that is appropriate to have, there is no universal limit. The key is that all segments fulfill the criteria listed above. Some rules of thumb on the maximum number of segments are to not have more segments than what your team can remember without a list, resulting in around seven to ten segments,[20] and that no segment should be less than 5 percent of the sample.[21]

HOW TO SEGMENT

There are, on a high level, two approaches for designing a new segmentation:

1. **Data-driven segmentation:** This approach starts with a large volume of customer data, such as usage and purchasing patterns, and clusters customers based on statistical similarities. While it can reveal unexpected insights, the results often become too technical or complex to use effectively in day-to-day decision-making (e.g., segments that cannot be observed in practice).

2. **Application-driven segmentation:** This approach begins with obvious or practical segments, based on how the segmentation will be used. It is then validated or refined with supporting data. This method is typically faster to implement and easier for internal teams to apply consistently. But beware of confirmation bias, where you interpret findings in ways that are preferential to existing beliefs, expectations, or hypotheses.

In most cases, the application-driven approach is preferred for its simplicity and practicality. Start by identifying the intended uses of your segmentation. As mentioned earlier, you may need different segmentations—or at least different levels of granularity—for different contexts, such as channel strategy, marketing, offer design, price model selection, discounting rules, sales enablement, and performance tracking.

In pricing specifically, segmentation should reveal differences in customer needs, perceived value, and willingness to pay. These insights help guide packaging decisions, set differentiated price points, and equip marketing and sales teams with tailored value arguments.[22]

You can design a segmentation in three steps:

1. **Identify differentiators:** These are the key variables where meaningful differences among customer groups exist and where treating customers differently makes sense. In the context of the AP automation example, this could include the outcome a customer is primarily trying to achieve (e.g., faster processing, eliminating manual work, stronger compliance, better visibility) and how much they are willing to pay.
2. **Determine dimensions:** These factors explain why the differentiators vary between customers. They typically reflect usage behavior or operational needs. For AP automation, relevant dimensions might include the number of invoices processed per year, the number of legal entities involved, the complexity of approval workflows, or which features and services are used (like PO matching or enterprise resource planning (ERP) integrations).
3. **Set descriptors:** These are observable or easily obtainable attributes that help you practically assign customers to segments. They add color and context to the dimensions and are often available in internal systems or market data. Common descriptors include company size (measured by employee count or revenue), industry (such as manufacturing or services), geography, or the customer's current tech stack (e.g., what ERP system they use or their level of digital maturity).

A helpful way to approach differentiators is through jobs-to-be-done[23]—focusing on the tasks customers want to accomplish. In AP automation, that could include processing invoices faster, matching purchase orders, or gaining better spend visibility. However, for pricing purposes, jobs alone aren't enough. You also need to consider willingness to pay, return on investment (ROI), and price sensitivity. The same need can yield different values for different customers. For instance, some customers may achieve greater cost savings using your solution, while others may be compelled to use your product due to regulatory requirements. For example, the AP automation solution offers integrations with multiple ERP systems. Some of these integrations were only provided, while others were offered by all competitors. This insight allowed them to charge a premium to customers requiring niche integrations.

The segmentation should not be an exercise for marketing only. Instead, assemble a cross-functional team covering at least marketing, sales, and product (but ideally also other relevant functions) to ensure the segmentation becomes both strategically sound and practically usable. Additionally, an effective segmentation must be grounded in a deep understanding of your customers. Surface-level groupings like size or industry can be a useful starting point, but they rarely capture underlying needs. Real insight comes from direct research—interviews, surveys, and conversations with internal teams who work with customers daily.

UNDERSTAND THE BUYING PROCESS

Understanding the buying process is crucial for setting effective packaging and pricing because it helps align your offering with customer decision-making behaviors and preferences. There are five stages of the buying process: need recognition, information search, evaluation of alternatives, purchase decision, and post-purchase behavior. These provide insights into what customers value, their price sensitivity, and how they compare options. Throughout the buying process, identify the key motivations and pain points of the buying persona, which may vary based on their role (e.g., user, influencer, decision-maker) and organization size. In particular, consider the decision-making dynamics within the organization, especially with enterprise versus small-to-medium-size businesses (SMBs). Identify who the primary stakeholders are and their roles in the process, as this can affect the length and complexity of the buying journey.

Here is an example of the buying process in the context of AP automation. In the first stage, need recognition occurs when a potential buyer, such as a finance manager or CFO, identifies inefficiencies in their current invoice-handling process. This recognition might stem from internal triggers, like late payments, high manual workload, or compliance risks. External triggers could include hearing about automation success in peer companies or being approached by a vendor. Recognizing the need for greater efficiency, accuracy, or scalability in AP processes sets the stage for the purchasing journey.

Next, in the information search stage, the buyer explores how AP automation solutions can solve their challenges. They may research online, read analyst reports, watch vendor demos, or ask peers in finance communities for recommendations. A controller might look up case studies from similar-sized businesses or industries to understand benefits like time savings, fraud reduction, or integration capabilities with their ERP system.

During the evaluation of alternatives, the buyer shortlists vendors based on key criteria, such as price models (e.g., per invoice or flat fee), feature set (e.g., invoice scanning, approval workflows, PO matching), integration with existing systems, user experience, and security compliance. For example, they may compare full-suite providers (i.e., tools with many capabilities across finance/procurement, also beyond AP automation) with more specialized tools (i.e., focusing on doing one thing well, such as AP automation). Vendors who communicate their differentiation, such as faster implementation, better support, or AI-driven invoice processing, stand out in this phase.

Once the buyer has weighed the options, they move to the purchase decision stage. At this point, stakeholders like IT, procurement, and legal may also get involved to finalize the deal. Factors like contract terms, pricing flexibility, implementation timelines, and stakeholder consensus influence the final decision. Offering a smooth buying experience, responsive sales support, and a clear onboarding plan can make or break the decision.

Finally, post-purchase behavior is key for long-term success. After implementation, the customer evaluates whether the AP automation solution delivers the promised efficiency gains and cost savings. If the system reduces invoice processing time significantly or eliminates late payment penalties, the buyer feels validated. Ongoing success can lead to renewals, expansion (e.g., adding more entities or invoice volume), or referrals, while a poor onboarding or unresolved issues can result in churn or negative feedback. Proactive customer success efforts and performance check-ins are crucial for retention and advocacy.

The buying process varies significantly based on customer size. For enterprise sales, the contract value is generally higher, sales cycles are longer, and the process involves numerous stakeholders and extended negotiations. Enterprise deals also frequently involve formal procurement processes, including request for proposals (RFPs) or tenders, which require detailed documentation, structured evaluation criteria, and adherence to strict timelines. On the other hand, sales to small- and medium-size customers typically feature smaller contract values, shorter sales cycles, fewer stakeholders, and minimal or no negotiations. Due to the differences in size, the enterprise deals are usually a bit riskier due to the cost of sales being higher than for a deal with a small- and medium-size customer. Depending on your process, you need to ensure you map out what is needed in terms of sales resources, competencies, and supporting material.

For certain products, especially expensive systems like ERP software, decisions are often made by a committee rather than an individual. When multiple stakeholders are involved, there are usually several budgets contributing. For example, in an ERP purchase, the IT department may fund infrastructure and technology, the finance team may pay for accounting features, and the operations team may budget for workflow and supply chain modules. Identifying the main buyer and other stakeholders helps tailor your packaging and pricing to capture value across all budgets.

Gain insights into the buying process using qualitative methods, such as interviews or surveys, to uncover the persona's preferences and decision-making process. Assess their typical buying behaviors, including how they seek and assess their buying criteria, i.e., factors influencing their choices such as price sensitivity and brand loyalty. These insights can inform tailored marketing and sales strategies, ensuring your messaging aligns with the specific needs and concerns of each persona. A thorough understanding of the buying process and personas enables you to enhance engagement, refine targeting, and ultimately drive more successful sales outcomes.

ANALYZE THE BUYING CRITERIA

When mapping out the buying process, it is important to understand the rationale for why a customer buys your product. Getting this understanding helps you understand what customers consider when assessing a product, which goes beyond individual features and includes, for example, security, ease of implementation, support level, etc. The rationale can be explained by the buying criteria. These criteria are based on how professional the buyer is, either formally or informally defined. Typically, there are no more than five to ten criteria that matter. Understanding these helps you in your pricing, sales, and marketing efforts.

A useful exercise is a modified version of the importance-performance analysis (IPA) by Martilla and James.[24] The exercise, which should ideally be done per segment, consists of listing all the buying criteria and then assessing both the importance for customers of each of them and your performance versus competitors. You will then get a picture like the one in Figure 2.2.

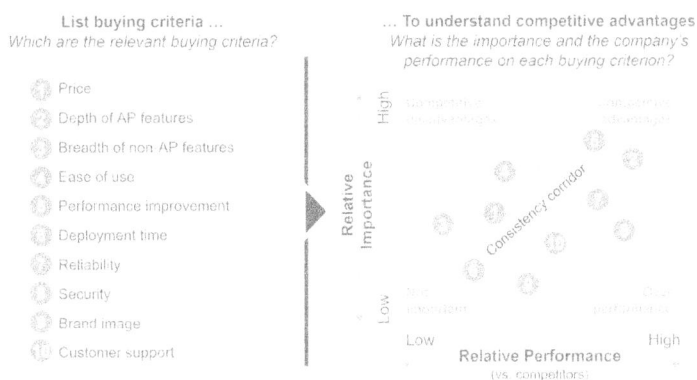

Figure 2.2: Example of an importance-performance exercise.

Typically, you aim to align your performance with the importance of each buying criterion, striving to excel in the most important areas while deprioritizing less important ones. However, in practice, performance and importance are often uncorrelated, with companies showing strong performance in areas that hold little value for the customer. From this analysis, you can categorize the criteria into four groups:

- **Competitive advantages:** These are the critical criteria where you outperform competitors. Emphasize these in your packaging, pricing, and sales strategies to appeal to the segment effectively.
- **Competitive disadvantages:** These are important criteria where your performance lags. Focus on improving these areas to remain competitive or downplay their importance during the sales process.
- **Overperformance:** These are less important criteria where your performance exceeds expectations. You can either scale back investments in these areas or work to elevate their perceived importance among customers.
- **Not important:** These are criteria of low importance where your performance is also low. While these can typically be left as-is, it's crucial to monitor them periodically to ensure they don't evolve into competitive disadvantages.

Based on experience, price is seldom the most important criterion. There are, on aggregate, typically at least two to four criteria that are more important than price. But with that said, this varies between segments. Some segments are more price-focused rather than value-focused. This is also why segmentation is key, so this variation in willingness to pay is understood and can be used in commercial decisions. In addition, the importance of certain criteria may differ throughout the ownership cycle. Price typically becomes less significant to customers after they have purchased the product, compared to before the purchase. This dynamic supports the "land and expand" strategy, where customers are initially acquired with a competitively priced basic offering and later upsold to premium packages at higher price points.

It's important to remember you can influence both the importance and performance of the criteria. Performance can be affected by investing in improving criteria where you lag or investing less in criteria where you overperform. Importance can be influenced by creating sales and marketing materials that highlight and emphasize the criteria where you overperform. Alternatively, it can be shaped by targeting customer segments that place high value on the criteria where you excel while placing less emphasis on areas where you perform less well. This process is a key part of defining your market position, which is covered in the final section of this chapter.

DETERMINE YOUR POSITION

At this point, you should have an overview of your segments and what your competitive advantages are versus competitors. On top of that, in Chapter 1, you have thought through where your company should be on key trade-offs. Given this information, you can determine your positioning.

Positioning is all about articulating the unique value your company can deliver to someone. April Dunford, a positioning expert, states, "Positioning defines how your product is the best in the world at delivering something, some value, that a well-defined set of customers cares a lot about."[25] In essence, positioning helps differentiate a company from its competitors, target and prioritize the right customers, and effectively communicate the company's value proposition. Highly focused, strategic positioning is critical to cutting through competitive noise and expanding your client base from early adopters into the mainstream.

An example is Veeva Vault, a content management platform targeting the life sciences and pharmaceutical industries. They focus on customers within a specific industry.[26]

When determining your positioning, start by identifying the specific segment or audience you want to target. Understand their needs, pain points, and desired outcomes. There are many ways to define your focus—by customer size, geography, industry, department, buyer, user, partner ecosystem, or within a specialized application area or tech stack. Once you've identified your niche, conduct a thorough competitive analysis. Consider what your customers would do if your product or service didn't exist. What alternatives would they turn to, and who are your main competitors? Identify what differentiates you and what gives you a competitive edge. Engage directly with current or prospective customers through interviews or surveys to understand their challenges, motivations, and the value they derive from your offering. These insights will enable you to clearly articulate the unique benefits and outcomes your product provides, which can then inform your value proposition and monetization model.

SUMMARY

- **Segment customers based on their needs:** Effective segmentation prioritizes customers based on their needs rather than just demographics. A strong segmentation model should be believable, actionable, differentiable, accessible, and substantial (BADAS) to guide marketing, sales, and pricing decisions effectively.

- **Understand your customers' buying process, involved stakeholders, and buying criteria:** Understanding the buying journey, from need recognition to post-purchase behavior, helps tailor packaging and pricing to customer decision-making dynamics. Mapping key buying criteria, such as ease of use, depth of features, or price, enables companies to optimize their positioning and sales strategies.

- **Determine your positioning:** A well-defined positioning strategy articulates the unique value a company delivers to a specific audience, differentiating it from competitors. By analyzing customer needs, competitive alternatives, and market fit, businesses can communicate their value proposition and strengthen their market presence.

CHAPTER 3

Channel Strategy

SELECT YOUR CHANNEL STRATEGY

When defining your overall strategy and customer segmentation, one key question will be about how to reach and acquire customers. This is where a channel strategy comes in. A channel strategy describes the methods and pathways through which a company sells and delivers its products or services to customers.

The channels you choose influence far more than just sales. They shape market reach, customer engagement, retention, and satisfaction, and they also have a direct impact on how products are packaged and priced. While this chapter does not cover all aspects of go-to-market strategy (for more details, see other sources[27]), it focuses specifically on how channel choices affect packaging and pricing.

MAIN SALES CHANNELS

There are, broadly speaking, three ways or channels for acquiring customers. The main channels are direct sales, indirect sales, and self-service. Direct sales involve selling directly to customers through an in-house sales team, either inbound (customers reaching out to you) or outbound (you reaching out to customers). This approach offers strong control over the sales process and requires a high level of customer interactions with different stakeholders, enabling companies to build direct relationships, gather valuable feedback, and better understand customer needs. It also allows firms to manage pricing, branding, and customer experience, fostering loyalty. However, direct sales come with higher customer acquisition costs, as building a dedicated team and engaging one-on-one can be resource intensive. Additionally, its reach may be limited, posing challenges in larger markets.

Indirect sales involve third-party partners selling the product on behalf of the company. These partners can take various forms:

- **"Sell-to" partners** embed your product within theirs and resell it, offering little to no visibility to their customers.
- **"Sell-through" partners**, like dealers or distributors, require you to enable their sales force without direct customer engagement.
- **"Sell-with" partners** involve collaborative selling, where you may join sales calls or act as a coach.
- **"Referral" partners** refer customers to you, leaving you with full customer ownership but paying a commission.

The relevance of the partner models depends on the product and the strategy, whether the product can be sold with the different partners and whether the strategy is to do so. There are also hybrid partners, which are combinations of these models. Indirect sales allow for rapid scaling and broader market access by leveraging partners' established customer bases and industry expertise, often reducing acquisition costs. However, this model limits control over customer interactions and brand messaging. Additionally, this can also require complex technical integrations and development of partner programs that can impact the price model.

Self-service sales allow customers to independently explore, trial, and purchase products without interacting with sales representatives. Variations of self-service in SaaS are product-led and community-led growth, which is explained later in this chapter. The self-service model is highly efficient, enabling customers to engage with the product at their own pace and often lowering overhead costs by minimizing the need for a sales team. It fits well when targeting small- and medium-size customers with less complex product/service needs. However, it may not suit complex products requiring significant support or training. Without proper guidance, customers might struggle to understand the product's capabilities, reducing conversion rates. Additionally, opportunities for upselling and cross-selling may be missed in a purely self-service environment.

CHANNEL SELECTION

A company can use a mix of direct, indirect, and self-service sales channels—or transition between them based on evolving business needs. By leveraging multiple strategies, you can maximize coverage of customer discovery and revenue opportunities. Each channel offers distinct benefits and challenges. The key is to identify which channels are the most and least effective for your business and allocate resources to those with the highest ROI.

Figure 3.1 lists common criteria for evaluating which channels to use and a general assessment of the performance of the channels. The trade-off is generally between the importance of personal interactions, engagement, and control, versus the importance of reach, costs, and scalability.

General assessment of channels based on key criteria

Criterion	Direct sales	Indirect sales	Self-service
Customer engagement	High	Medium	
Packaging and pricing complexity	High	Medium	
Market reach	Medium	High	High
Scalability needs		Medium	High
Cost implications		Medium	High
Control over the sales process	High		Medium
Feedback speed		Medium	High

Performance: ⚙ High   ⚙ Medium   Low

Figure 3.1. General assessment of the different channels.

The factors to consider when selecting channels are described further below, sorted based on how important those factors generally are (from the generally most to least important factor):

- **Customer engagement preferences:** Direct and indirect sales foster strong relationships and loyalty through personal interactions, essential for complex or consultative sales. Self-service appeals to customers who prioritize autonomy and quick decision-making, enabling them to navigate the buying process independently. The key is to align your sales model with how your customers prefer to buy. Some require trust-building through human interaction, while others expect a seamless, digital-first experience with minimal friction.
- **Packaging and pricing complexity:** Complex offerings and pricing requiring detailed explanations are best suited for direct or indirect sales, where sales reps can provide tailored support and address concerns. Straightforward packaging and pricing benefit from self-service models, allowing

customers to independently complete purchases, appealing to efficiency-focused buyers. Matching the sales model to how your customer wants to explore and evaluate solutions helps reduce friction and improve conversion.

- **Market reach and customer segments:** For broad markets, leverage indirect sales to access new segments without significantly expanding your internal sales force. For niche or smaller markets, direct sales provide focused engagement to build trust and credibility. Self-service models enable scalable, low-cost expansion by reaching large audiences with minimal overhead.
- **Scalability needs:** Direct sales are challenging to scale rapidly due to the need for more resources. Indirect sales scale efficiently through partnerships, while self-service excels in automated scalability, accommodating large user volumes with minimal incremental costs.
- **Cost implications:** Direct sales incur high operational costs, including salaries, commissions, and training. Indirect sales lower internal costs but introduce partner commissions. Self-service is the most cost-efficient, relying mainly on technology investments and platform maintenance.
- **Control over the sales process:** Direct sales offer full control over customer experience and messaging, ensuring alignment with your brand. Indirect sales rely on partners, which can introduce variability in brand representation. Self-service requires intuitive interfaces and clear communication to maintain a consistent experience without direct engagement.
- **Feedback speed:** Direct sales provide immediate insights from customer interactions, allowing quick adjustments to the sales strategy. Indirect sales depend on partner reporting, which can delay feedback. Self-service offers data on conversion rates, site visitors, etc., but provides limited qualitative feedback in terms of win/loss reasons.

When using multiple channels, it's crucial to clearly define which channels will target specific customer segments and which products will be offered through each. Creating a visual overview, such as Figure 3.2, can help provide clarity by mapping out products, customer segments, and channels.

During this process, watch for potential channel conflicts that may arise when the same products are sold to the same customers through different channels. This can lead to competition between channels, often resulting in price undercutting and revenue loss. If there is a risk of channel conflict, establish guidelines on how these conflicts should be resolved, such as through differentiated pricing, exclusive product offerings, or channel-specific customer targeting. Alternatively, revise your strategy by limiting certain products or customer groups to specific channels.

Key questions in the channel strategy

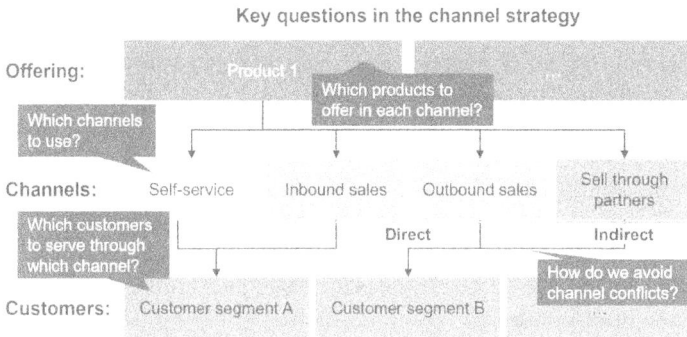

Figure 3.2. Outline on how to reach your customers and corresponding questions.

DIRECT SALES CONSIDERATIONS

To succeed with pricing in direct sales, several key considerations must be addressed. First, gaining deep insights into customer needs, pain points, and the buying process (see Chapter 2) is crucial. This understanding enables a more tailored sales approach and helps position the offering around the value it delivers rather than just the features or price.

Building a capable and confident sales team is equally important. Invest in the right tools (e.g., CRM systems), training, and value-based sales collateral to equip the team for success. Focus on enabling value-selling rather than price-selling, ensuring that your team can communicate and defend the value behind the pricing.

To maintain pricing discipline, introduce structured discount guidelines and escalation paths—especially for large or complex deals—to prevent margin erosion. Support this with an incentive structure that aligns with your business goals (see Chapter 1), rewarding behaviors that support both growth and profitability.

Ensure regular knowledge-sharing between salespeople through structured forums, internal playbooks, or deal debriefs. This encourages alignment in messaging, objection handling, and proven tactics.

Finally, foster close collaboration between sales and pricing teams. Create feedback loops to continuously refine packaging and pricing based on frontline insights. This alignment helps both teams stay responsive to shifts in customer needs, competitive moves, and deal dynamics. For more on price governance and communication, see Chapters 7 and 8.

INDIRECT SALES CONSIDERATIONS

Success in indirect sales depends on selecting the right partners and building a structured, well-managed partner program.

Start by identifying partners that align with your product, target market, and customer needs. Look for companies that serve similar customer segments with complementary solutions, creating cross-selling and co-marketing opportunities. Prioritize partners with strong reputations, proven sales capabilities, and established customer relationships. Evaluate how well they can integrate your solution into their existing offering and go-to-market strategy.

Once selected, design a partner program with a scalable structure (i.e., a program that can be used for all partners). Define commission (there are many other terms used, including discounts or incentives) for the partner roles (e.g., "sell to," "sell through," or "referral"). Adjust commissions to reflect the level of effort and risk each partner takes on. Introduce performance-based incentives, such as tiered commissions or volume-based bonuses to motivate partner engagement, customer acquisition, and upselling efforts. Just remember to design the program to reflect your business objectives.

Support is key. Provide comprehensive onboarding and training so partners can effectively position and sell your solution. Equip them with co-branded marketing materials, clear product documentation, and easy access to value-selling resources (see Chapter 7 for value-selling material). Ensure pricing updates and packaging changes are communicated promptly and consistently.

Designate a dedicated partner manager to own the program internally. This person should act as the central point of contact, monitor partner performance, and lead regular check-ins. A strong internal owner helps enforce pricing discipline, encourages knowledge sharing, and ensures your partners are aligned with your monetization strategy.

SELF-SERVICE CONSIDERATIONS

When offering a self-service sales model, the focus should be on delivering a seamless, intuitive user experience. The product must be easy to navigate and onboard, even as complexity grows with more features or customer segments. Strong user experience and onboarding are essential to drive adoption without direct sales involvement.

Make pricing clear and transparent. Display pricing tiers and feature comparisons on your website to help users make informed decisions (see more in Chapter 7). Avoid hidden fees to build trust and reduce friction.

Usage-based pricing often works well in self-service models, as it directly links cost to value received, making it easier for users to justify spending. Support self-sufficiency with resources, such as a knowledge base, community forum, or onboarding checklist. Empower users to manage their accounts and upgrades—creating a frictionless path to expand usage and increase average revenue per account (ARPA).

As part of your pricing, consider whether to implement a freemium model or offer free trials to lower entry barriers and encourage users to explore your product. Generally, freemium provides basic services for free while charging for advanced features, making it suitable for generating a large user base. Free trials, on the other hand, typically offer users a full-featured experience for a limited time, helping them evaluate whether the product delivers sufficient value. Freemium works well when:

- Free users can be monetized directly (e.g., through ads or other fees) or indirectly (e.g., by improving the user experience, enabling network effects, adding community content, etc.).
- There is a clear upsell path from free to paid plans, where the paid plans are differentiated and provide significant additional value (see Chapter 4).
- The product is complex or requires interaction to drive appeal.
- Supporting the free version incurs low resource costs.
- The primary goal is user acquisition or platform engagement.
- There is a large potential user base to monetize.
- Product usage can drive virality or network effects.

In contrast, a free trial is effective when:

- The goal is increased conversion to paying customers rather than an overall user acquisition.
- The core value proposition is evident through product use.
- A key acquisition challenge is driving engagement.
- Significant value can be realized in a short time (days or weeks).
- The product is simple to use.
- Full-featured access is critical to demonstrating product value.

The choice between freemium and free trials depends on your business objectives and whether the criteria above are met. Once chosen, it's crucial to design packaging, pricing, and the sales process to optimize conversion rates from free to paying customers.

Beyond initial acquisition, offer incentives to encourage upgrades, such as discounts, reverse trials (providing temporary full-feature access), or time-limited promotions. Additionally, prepare reengagement offers to win back lapsed users, further maximizing long-term growth and revenue.

PRODUCT- AND COMMUNITY-LED GROWTH

Some variations of the self-service strategy in SaaS that have gained popularity are product-led growth (PLG) and community-led growth (CLG). Both shift the focus from traditional sales-led models to user experience and peer-driven influence, placing the product and community at the center of customer acquisition and expansion. These models have some direct implications for how packaging and pricing should be designed, beyond what is described in the section on self-service (see previous section).

PLG relies on the product to drive acquisition, retention, and expansion. Users onboard themselves, explore features independently, and experience value before engaging with sales—if they do at all. This model builds on the principles of self-service: intuitive onboarding, transparent pricing, and clear upgrade paths are foundational. Freemium models, free trials, and usage-based pricing help reduce barriers to entry and support a "land and expand" approach. Packaging should reflect this journey, starting with a value-rich entry plan that invites trial and adoption, and then scaling through tiered plans or modular add-ons that reward increased usage or organizational needs.

CLG complements PLG by leveraging an engaged community to build trust, drive awareness, and encourage adoption. Through peer support, user-generated content, and social proof, community-led growth enhances credibility, especially in technical or developer-oriented markets. Packaging and pricing need to serve both sides of the market: contributors and decision-makers. For community users, this may mean free or low-cost access to foster engagement and experimentation. For enterprises, premium tiers should offer enhanced features, such as administrative tools, security controls, and prioritized support.

Where relevant, CLG pricing can also reflect the value of community assets, such as insights, integrations, or talent pipelines, embedded in the broader offering. However, monetization must be approached with care: overly aggressive tactics risk alienating the community that drives growth. Nonmonetary rewards like recognition, early access, or exclusive content often do more to incentivize engagement than discounts or commissions.

Ultimately, both PLG and CLG depend on packaging and pricing that scale with customer maturity, enabling users to adopt and grow at their own pace. As with self-service models, simplicity, transparency, and flexibility are essential.

SUMMARY

- **Select preferred sales channel(s) per segment and market:** The three main sales channels—direct, indirect, and self-service—each come with distinct benefits and trade-offs in terms of control, cost, scalability, and customer engagement, and should be selected or combined based on product complexity, buyer preferences, and market strategy.
- **Identify and mitigate potential channel conflicts:** When using multiple channels, clearly define which segments and products each channel targets, and proactively manage potential conflicts with strategies like differentiated pricing, exclusive offerings, or channel-specific focus.
- **Select partners and design a partner program (if you use indirect sales):** Choose partners that align with your product and customer base, then build a scalable program with clear roles, expectations, and incentives.
- **Consider freemium or a free trial (if you use self-service):** Choose between freemium and free trials based on your goals—freemium works best for driving broad user acquisition and engagement, while free trials are suited for converting high-intent users. In both cases, ensure packaging and pricing are designed to support seamless conversion to paid plans.
- **Account for key considerations for each channel:** Each sales channel has its own considerations for how to set up the packaging, pricing, and sales process. Ensure that you learn more about the considerations and incorporate them in the work ahead.

CHAPTER 4

Offering Model

OFFERING DESIGN

After having determined the customer segmentation and the channel strategy, the next step is to use that information to design an offering based on customers' needs, how they discover and buy the product, and which channels the product is sold through.

ADDRESSING KEY PACKAGING CHALLENGES

Packaging issues typically fall into three categories that signal a need for redesign. The first issue arises with a one-size-fits-all offering, where some customers pay too much or too little compared to their willingness to pay. This happens because customers derive varying levels of value from the product, yet the price remains uniform. In such cases, the price is usually set between the highest and lowest willingness to pay, which fails to fully capture the product's value for different segments. Addressing this requires introducing differentiated packaging, such as a Good/Better/Best model, to better align pricing with value delivered.

The second issue occurs at the other extreme—a "build-your-own" model where customers choose from numerous products and add-ons. While flexible, this approach often results in high acquisition costs and customers purchasing less than they need due to decision fatigue. Simplifying the offering by clustering features or transitioning to, for example, a Good/Better/Best structure can reduce complexity, making it easier for customers to choose while improving overall sales efficiency.

The third issue arises when there is some differentiation, but the packages either include too many features or features that are not relevant to many of the target customers. Typical symptoms include friction, such as low conversion rates or high discounting for certain packages. Another common problem is too many customers opt for the most basic package because it includes too many features, making it suitable for too broad an audience. To address these situations, conduct a study to assess the value and adoption of the various features (as discussed later in this chapter) and use these insights to refine and update the packages.

LONGLIST OFFERING MODEL CONTENT

The first step in designing the offering model is to get transparency on what you can include. This exercise brings clarity on what features, and through them what benefits, you can offer your customers. What you need to do is to longlist key features that you are offering. It is important here to think through all the aspects of the offering; there are the obvious components:

- **Core product features:** The features included in the main products sold. These are usually the main reasons for customers to buy from you.
- **Add-on product feature:** Features that are too niche to include in the current core products.

But some features are often forgotten and could contribute. Depending on your product, the impact can be significant:

- **Support and service-level agreements (SLAs):** Features related to support given to customers, e.g., by phone and email, but also uptime, response times, support hours, languages, etc.
- **Transactional offering:** Features that are mainly sold on a pay-as-you-go basis today, such as payment services, e-signatures, know-your-customer (KYC) checks, or other elements.
- **Professional services:** Features such as product coaching, customer success, training, and development. These are usually offered on a time and material basis.
- **Other features:** There are often more features than you might think. For example, if there is something related to customization, data update frequency, being compliant with certain industry standards, etc.

When listing your features, think about the benefits that the features bring, because customers don't buy products; they buy the benefits that the products bring them. An example of this is the iPod, which wasn't sold as "a 5 GB MP3 player," but rather "one thousand songs in your pocket." What this means in the example of the AP automation solution, you can see in Figure 4.1. Their customers don't buy features, such as "Capture" or "Approval workflow." They buy the benefits of automating data entry or speeding up approvals as part of the invoice handling.

Feature	Benefit
Capture	Automate data entry, reduce errors, and save time from repetitive tasks
Purchase order matching	Ensure accurate invoicing, prevent overpayments, and maintain control
Payment module	Streamline payment processing, improve cash flow, and reduce administrative tasks
Approval workflow	Speed up approvals, boost compliance, and minimize fraud risk
AI-assisted posting and workflow	Automate transactions and workflows, improve both accuracy and efficiency
...	...
Standard support	Enjoy quick assistance for everyday issues, keeping your operations smooth
Extended support	Receive expert help and faster resolution for more complex challenges

Figure 4.1. Example of features and their corresponding benefits for the AP automation example.

SELECT PACKAGING APPROACH

The former CEO of Netscape, Jim Barksdale, once famously proclaimed, "There are only two ways I know of to make money—bundling and unbundling."[28] In principle, that is correct. However, there is a spectrum of bundling, going from being completely bundled to completely unbundled.

There are generally five archetypes of packaging approaches,[29] which are displayed in Figure 4.2. These packages vary in three dimensions: the flexibility versus customers' needs, how easy they are to understand, and the development investments needed. Generally, the flexibility to cater to customer needs increases with the number of packages, but so does the complexity, which makes it more difficult to understand the full offering. Furthermore, more packages typically mean higher development and maintenance costs. Below is a summary of the different archetypes.

Figure 4.2. The five packaging archetypes.

One-size-fits-all (or often called "all-you-can-eat") means you have one offering with all features. This has the benefit of being easy to understand but has the disadvantage of not having the flexibility to cater for differences in needs. This setup is suitable if you want to drive encouragement and focus on maximum simplicity. Due to everything being included, the prices could easily end up being perceived as expensive for customers who only need a few features. An example of a company with one-size-fits-all packaging is the business and financial information platform Bloomberg Terminal.[30]

Use case packages target specific customer types. It simplifies the purchase process and helps target multiple customer segments. This works if benefits/features are more important to specific customers than to others and if those differences do not tend to change over time. One example of use case packages is LinkedIn, which sells different packages depending on the user's role, for example, job seeker, recruiter, salesperson, etc.

Good/Better/Best is a line-up of packages with increasing/more feature functionality, normally three or four.[31] It has the benefit of providing some flexibility while still being quite predetermined. The structure forces trade-offs on value versus price, and offerings can grow with customer needs. This works best when it's realistic to differentiate only using features. Good/Better/Best is likely one of the most common archetypes[32] and is used by, for example, the communication platform Slack or the survey platform SurveyMonkey.

Platform plus packages consist of a core platform with some core features and then packages as add-ons that target different use cases. This setup is simple but can still target customers with varying willingness to pay. It is, however, important that the platform contains features that all customers find valuable in order to justify the setup. Furthermore, the complexity of selling all the add-ons will still be in place. This setup is offered by Salesforce, which offers a CRM platform and then multiple add-ons targeting specific use cases or industries.

Build-your-own (or sometimes called "à la carte") is a flexible package that offers the maximum choice and enables self-selection by unique needs and willingness to pay. This is most suitable for customers who can make informed decisions based on needs/willingness to pay and if customers have wide-ranging needs and value maximum flexibility. The challenge is it can be overwhelming to select the features, as well as there's a risk of cherry picking specific features. An example of a company with build-your-own packaging is the cloud technology company Oracle.

The five packaging options listed above are just archetypes. It is possible to come up with your own package types. For example, a platform differentiated into Good/Better/Best packages with add-ons on top, or functional packages with multiple add-ons. Just keep in mind what complexity your customers and your sales channels can handle, which is part of the strategic trade-offs discussed in Chapter 1 (Business Objectives).

The approach that best suits you depends on your customers' needs, how they discover and buy your product, and which channels you sell through. Self-service sales are preferably combined with a simple packaging approach to make it easier to understand the offering. While a sales-led process, both with your own sales team or with partners, can be a bit more complex depending on the product, the customer, and the skills of the sales teams.

HOW TO ALLOCATE FEATURES TO PACKAGES

The process continues by assigning features to the distinct packages, after first listing the features and selecting a packaging strategy. The configuration is done by understanding customer adoption and the customers' perceived value of each feature. Depending on the degree of value and adoption, features can be categorized in four groups as seen in Figure 4.3.[33] To make the concept more concrete, a burger menu is used as a comparison.

- **High value/high adoption, "must-haves"**: Features are the main reason for your purchase. These features have a high value to most customers. In comparison with the burger menu, this is the protein.
- **Low value/high adoption, "nice to haves"**: Features have a medium/low value to most customers. These are features that aren't the main reason for buying in the first place, but if they are included with a package discount, they are also purchased. These features are, for example, the fries and the soda in the burger menu.
- **High value/low adoption, "add-ons"**: Features have a low value for most customers but have a very high value for a selected number of customers.

These features should generally be sold as add-ons. This is, for example, the coffee that is not included in the burger menu. Some people would appreciate having it included, but most do not want to have it included.

- **Low value/low adoption, "don't needs"**: These should generally be sold as add-ons if they have a value that justifies a separate price and the additional offering complexity, or, if the feature is technically necessary and of very low value, it might be included in all packages without being explicitly mentioned. You should also consider whether to offer some of these features.

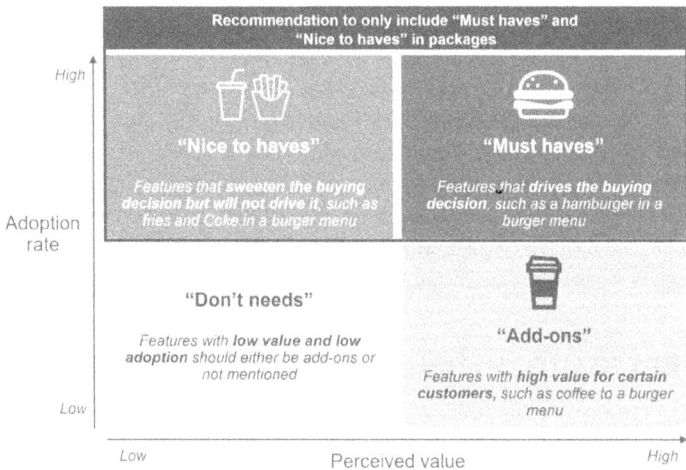

Figure 4.3. The four feature categories.

The key is to only include "must-have" and "nice-to-have" features in the packages. A common approach is that some "add-on" features are included in all packages for simplicity. This may seem to be a good idea, but the problem is that when you include features that customers don't want, they will likely ask for discounts because they don't want to pay for features they see little to no value in.

The feature categorization is conducted by first longlisting all features that can be differentiated, which is described earlier in this chapter. Then elementary "table-stakes" features are sorted out—they are features that need to be included in the product to fulfill its purposes. These are not necessary to include in the categorization because they must be in place for the product to be considered complete. The remaining features should then be included in surveys/interviews with current and/or potential customers to understand the categorization. For example, in a car, table-stakes features would include essentials like the steering wheel and airbags, which are considered standard. In contrast, differentiating features—those used to distinguish between packages—might include a panoramic roof, self-parking capabilities, or adaptive cruise control, which offer unique value and help set certain models apart.

An example is shown in Figure 4.4 for an AP automation solution. The selected packaging approach was Good/Better/Best because it reflects the variations in customer needs, which are driven based on automation needs (rather than use case specific needs). Furthermore, the hypothesis was that the platform plus packages approach would be too complex to sell for both their own sales team and partners.

Figure 4.4 shows the aggregated responses to different features for customers characterized as having a low or high level of automation. Based on the results, it is possible to conclude that a basic offering (Good package) would include capture, document workflow and archive, approval workflow, insights platform, and standard support. While a premium offering (Best package) would include everything besides automation coach, contract management, and the payment module. The Better package is a configuration between these two (not shown here to reduce complexity in the figure). Automation coach, contract management, and payment module are future add-ons due to being valued by just a subset of customers.

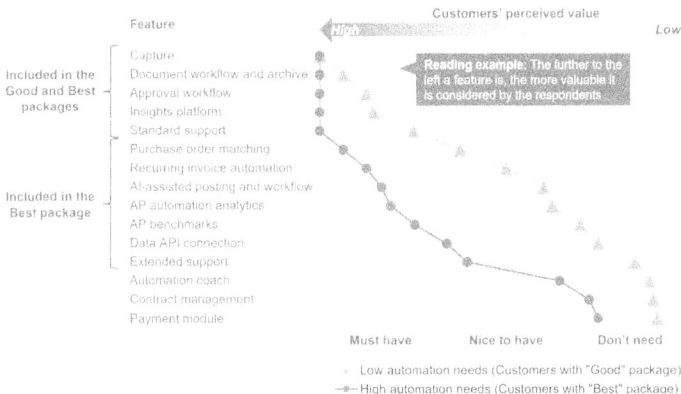

Figure 4.4. Feature rating of an AP automation solution. This exercise should be done to consider the selected packaging approach.

If you have a sizable number of customers already, you can complement the above with analyses of usage and sales data. From this data, you could analyze which features are bought and/or used by different customer segments. This provides clues for which features to combine into packages. In addition, you can also review historical data to see in which order products are sold.

In the same survey/interviews where you ask questions to determine feature categorization, it is also helpful to bring concrete concepts that interviewees can comment on and react to. A cross-functional team, covering at least marketing, product, and sales, should be able to create mockups of packages you can show the respondents. Then you could ask questions such as:

- Do you understand the packages?
- Are the packages logical?
- Which package would you choose?
- What would you add/remove from your favorite package?

Based on the exercises above, you should get a good understanding of what features to allocate to which packages and which features to offer as add-ons.

DIFFERENTIATION BETWEEN PACKAGES

The main differentiation between packages is typically included features, but there are more tactics for creating differences among packages. You can differentiate (in order of how common they are):

- **Included features:** A customer has different features depending on the package. For example, an extensive analytics module is only included in the better package.
- **The included volume:** There are caps on how much volume/users are included in each package. For example, you must have a better package if you have more than five users. This is also called a "fencing metric" and is described further in Chapter 5 (Price Model).
- **Prices of transactions:** The price per transaction, hour, etc. differs between packages, with lower prices for more premium packages. For example, a customer with the better package gets a 10 percent discount on professional services/development versus a customer with the good package.
- **Available add-ons:** A customer has different add-ons depending on the package. For example, a customer can only buy a data export/API with the better package.

Using multiple or all of these tactics together/concurrently increases the complexity of your offering. If you want to minimize complexity, start by differentiating packages by included features, as it offers the most tangible and intuitive distinction for customers. If additional differentiation is needed, limiting the included volume is a common tactic (but each volume metric used increases complexity).

However, sometimes greater differentiation between packages is necessary, requiring the use of additional tactics. When doing so, ensure the differentiation aligns with the customer's needs to limit friction, such as customers feeling nickel-and-dimed due to being forced into upgrades they do not see the full value in. For example, if packages include a set volume of usage, those levels should correlate with the demand for other features within the same package. Similarly, when differentiating the prices of transactions, customers in premium packages should benefit from the associated discounts.

UPSELL PATH DEFINITION

From numerous packaging and pricing projects, we have repeatedly seen a difference in the willingness to pay for customers before and after they have become a customer.[34] Before the initial purchase, when the customer hasn't really tested the product and fully understood the value, the willingness to pay is lower. But when a customer has used the product and knows how it works, the willingness to pay increases. This is why an offering model should include a landing offering with the basic features, targeting new customers with low willingness to pay, and then having upsell paths to more premium packages and add-ons.

When designing the offering model, it is key to think about the upsell paths from the beginning. This is done by understanding what features customers typically will need in the beginning and what they will need in the future, and in what order customers typically buy the features. It is important to find the right balance between the basic plan and the upgrade, based on your analysis of the adoption and perceived value of the features. Your product should be interesting enough in the basic plan, but the incentive to upgrade is also high enough. Also ensure the price differences for upgrading to a more premium package and/or adding new add-ons are not deferring. Finally, incorporate the upsell path information into the onboarding process and/or in later sales dialogues.

For example, in Microsoft Office 365, when users sign up for these services, they are initially offered the basic or lower-tier plans. But, in both the sign-up process and throughout their user journey, they are encouraged to upgrade to premium plans with more features and storage capacity. Companies should utilize the upsell path to move their customers from a lower-tier subscription to a higher-tier subscription, thereby increasing the overall customer lifetime value.

OTHER CONSIDERATIONS IN THE PACKAGE DESIGN

When designing packages, there are considerations to keep in mind. Below are a few considerations that may easily be forgotten in the design process.

- **Differentiate support:** Some customers have high requirements for support. Differentiating support is common and includes the introduction of premium support, with, for example, faster response time, better availability, etc.
- **Include services:** When including professional services in packages, it is crucial to clearly define what is included to manage customer expectations and control costs. Given the cost implications, a thorough understanding of the associated service costs is essential. Key considerations for bundling services are outlined in Chapter 9 (Special Topics).
- **Bundle hardware:** Bundling hardware requires an understanding of the costs of the included hardware. Considerations for bundling hardware are summarized in Chapter 9 (Special Topics).
- **Third-party products:** Some features may be external and used with permission and a potential royalty/fee. External products need special care in terms of thinking about the current and future costs (i.e., potential increases or decreases). If the cost is high versus the product price and there is unpredictability regarding the development, it is safer to leave the third-party products as add-ons.
- **New features:** When adopting a new offering model, think through how new features in the roadmap will fit into it. Determine, for example, whether a feature should be included in all packages or just in certain packages or add-ons.

SUMMARY

- **Longlist available features and their corresponding benefits:** Start by identifying all potential features, including core functionalities, add-ons, services, and support, and then map each to the benefits they deliver, as customers buy outcomes, not features.
- **Determine packaging approach based on customer needs and channel strategy:** Choose from packaging models like one-size-fits-all, use case packages, Good/Better/Best, platform plus packages, or build-your-own. Decide your approach by balancing customer flexibility with ease of understanding, and consider your customers' needs and your sales channels.
- **Design packages based on feature value and adoption:** Categorize features by value and adoption (including must-have, nice-to-have, add-ons, and don't need) to determine what to include in the packages versus what to offer as add-ons. Use customer interviews, surveys, and data analysis to inform the feature categorization.
- **Define the upsell path for customers:** Customer willingness to pay increases after adoption, so design your offering with a basic landing package and clear upsell paths to premium packages and features. Plan these paths early based on typical customer needs over time, and ensure pricing and onboarding support upgrades without friction.
- **Consider all components in the offering (e.g., support, services, hardware, and third-party products):** When designing packages, consider all possible components and their implications. For example, define included services and evaluate the cost implications of bundling hardware or third-party features. Additionally, plan for how future features will fit into the offering model.

CHAPTER 5

Price Model

THE PURPOSE OF A PRICE MODEL

After you have strategic considerations in place, as well as an understanding of what the offering will look like, it is time to determine the price model. Selecting the right price model is critical because how you charge often has a greater impact than what you charge. Choosing the wrong model can lead to scenarios like the one on the far left in Figure 5.1, where customers who get more value from your product are paying less. The goal is to shift toward the middle scenario or ideally the far-right scenario, where pricing aligns with the value customers receive: the more value a customer derives from your product, the more they pay.[35]

Figure 5.1: Different scenarios regarding alignment between ARR and perceived value.

In theory, this may seem easy, but there are key considerations to keep in mind. To begin with, you must understand what an efficient price model is. In a perfect or ideal world, the price model should fulfill these criteria:

- **Value capture:** Prices should scale with customer growth and usage.
- **Ease of implementation:** Pricing must be easy to track, monitor, and communicate.
- **Tracks with cost:** Costs should scale proportionally or slower than revenue.
- **Acceptability and fairness:** Pricing should be transparent, competitive, and free of hidden fees.
- **Predictability:** A stable structure helps customers plan budgets and avoid surprises.
- **Flexibility:** Customers should be able to adjust services to fit their needs and budgets.
- **Customer adoption:** Pricing should encourage adoption, enabling future upsells.

These criteria ensure price models bring value to both your company and your customers, and should guide the selection of all components of the price model. There are four components of a price model, which are illustrated in Figure 5.2. These are:

1. **Metric:** What you charge for, such as per user, per invoice, or per gigabyte.
2. **Modality:** When you charge, either upfront as a license-based or a token-based model, or in arrears as a pay-as-you-go model.
3. **Granularity:** How many units of the metric you pay for, either per individual unit (e.g., one, two, three, etc.) or for a tier of units (e.g., one through five, six through ten, etc.).
4. **Structure:** How the price scales with the number of units of the metrics. Including whether there should be a linear or digressive (i.e., the unit price decreases with the number of units) pricing, or if there should be a minimum and/or maximum.

Note, however, there is not yet a standardized naming of different price model components.[36] To give some examples, the music-streaming service Spotify charges per individual user upfront (for the paid versions) and charges the same price for each user (although there are special plans for people in the same household).[37] A more complex example is the delivery management solution nShift that charges based on the number of parcels shipped per year and the number of carriers used.[38] nShift has a license-based setup paid upfront, where the prices for parcels are sold in tiers (1–1,000, 1,001–2,500, etc.), while the carriers are sold per unit. The parcels follow a digressive price curve, where the price per parcel decreases with an increasing number of parcels, while carriers have the same unit price for each added carrier.

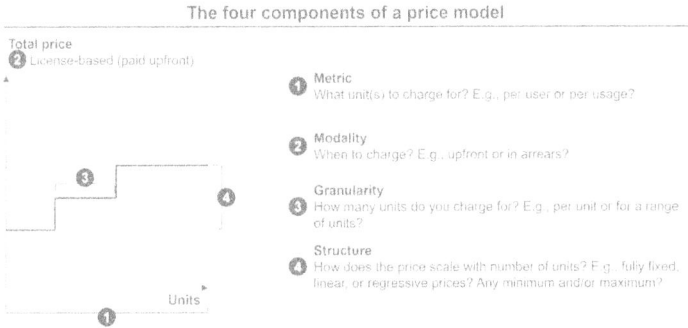

Figure 5.2: The four components of a price model: metric, modality, granularity, and structure.

This chapter will describe the four components, then mention how to assess a price model, and lastly describe other key considerations regarding price models. Initially, the focus is on the price model for the main product. Price model considerations for add-ons and secondary products are described later in this chapter.

METRIC

Historically, pricing has been limited by what could be measured. Products like machines and equipment were typically sold transactionally, not because customers necessarily wanted to own them but because ownership was the only practical basis for pricing. Leasing later emerged as an alternative, but it was still too imprecise. Leasing something for a day could lead to vastly different levels of usage and perceived value. Today, affordable sensors have largely removed those barriers, making it easy to track actual usage and enabling price models based on consumption, for example, charging per hour of actual usage of the machine.

Digitalization has further transformed pricing by allowing businesses to measure many more dimensions, enabling pricing to better reflect the value customers receive. A key yet often overlooked aspect of modern pricing is the choice of metric. User-based pricing has long been the default, originating in the era of perpetual software licenses when software was sold on physical media for on-premises use. However, in today's cloud-based world, this model doesn't always align with the value delivered. A wider range of price metrics is now available, offering more flexibility to match pricing with usage or outcomes.

Price metrics can have two different roles: either they are used as a monetization metric or a fencing metric. The monetization metric, also called the primary metric, is the main basis on which you charge. That is what you use to measure the units for the overall price. The fencing metric, also called the secondary metric, is used for limiting the full product functionality. This could have limitations, for example, "up to five users" for a package. If you surpass it, you have to move to a larger package. The purpose of this metric, besides limiting functionalities, is to partly force customers to upgrade to another package, but it's also to help prevent gaming or behavioral distortion in the usage (e.g., users sharing one login because the price is per user).

Furthermore, metrics can also be classified into three categories, depending on what they measure: input-based, process-based, and outcome-based. Generally, these categories vary in terms of whether they are aligned with cost or value, easy or hard to measure, and internally or externally focused. These are shown in Figure 5.3. with some practical examples.[39] Note, however, that classifying price metrics into the categories isn't always straightforward. For example, metrics like "invoices processed" could be seen as either a process or an outcome metric, depending on how the value is framed. Similarly, the classification of a metric like "number of users" varies by product. For an AP automation solution, it serves as an input metric, while for social media platforms (e.g., Facebook or LinkedIn), it functions as an outcome metric, since the value lies in active users driving engagement and ad revenue.

A summary of the three categories is:

- **Input-based metrics:** You charge customers based on what customers put in or consume, such as the number of users, API calls, or storage capacity. These metrics are simple to track and explain but may not always reflect the actual value customers derive.
- **Process-based metrics:** Pricing is based on what the customer does with your product—the actions or activities performed. Some examples are the number of invoices processed, workflows automated, or survey responses. These metrics capture customer engagement but can add billing complexity if activities aren't well-defined or predictable.

- **Outcome-based metrics:** Customers pay based on the results or success they achieve from using your product, such as revenue generated, cost savings achieved, or leads converted. These align closely with perceived value but are harder to measure and attribute directly to the product.

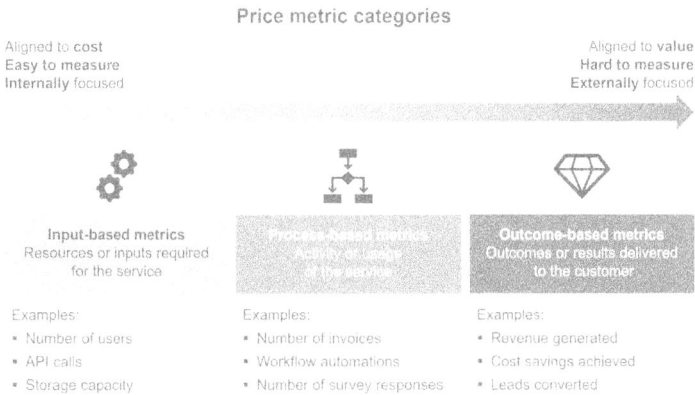

Price metric categories

Aligned to cost		Aligned to value
Easy to measure		Hard to measure
Internally focused		Externally focused

Input-based metrics	Process-based metrics	Outcome-based metrics
Resources or inputs required for the service	Activity or usage of the service	Outcomes or results delivered to the customer

Examples:	Examples:	Examples:
• Number of users	• Number of invoices	• Revenue generated
• API calls	• Workflow automations	• Cost savings achieved
• Storage capacity	• Number of survey responses	• Leads converted

Figure 5.3. Examples of the three metric types.

Ideally, you want to choose a metric as far to the right as possible on the value scale (see Figure 5.2), meaning an outcome metric. AI tools increasingly facilitate this by enabling pricing tied to outcomes, such as resolved customer support tickets or flagged fraudulent transactions. However, objectively measuring these metrics and securing customer acceptance can be challenging. For instance, an AP automation provider preferred to charge based on a percentage of total spend, which would have reflected the solution's value in reducing risks like invoice errors, inefficiencies, and fraud. However, this was not accepted by customers, leading to a price-per-invoice model as a more suitable compromise. Further details on price model evaluation criteria are provided later in this chapter.

Another consideration when selecting metrics is determining how many to use. Based on experience, using no more than two monetization/primary metrics strikes the balance between maximizing monetization and managing complexity. In many cases, a single metric is sufficient. However, add-ons can have their own price metrics if they better reflect the value delivered to the customer.

MODALITY

Another factor to think about is how the price model works in practice. The main models are license-based, pay-as-you-go, and credit-based models. The main differences are when you pay, i.e., upfront or in arrears, and if unused volume will carry over to the next billing cycle or not.

Let's start with license-based models. These are billed upfront by customers for the right to use a certain volume during a specific period. For example, the customer pays for ten users or processing ten thousand invoices, although they may only use four or eight thousand. In other words, unused volume will expire and not carry over to the next billing cycle. If a customer needs more users or invoices, they have to buy a larger volume. This model is predictable for both the customer and the company, but there may be some discontent from customers that they pay for volume that they don't use.

The pay-as-you-go model is where customers use a certain volume before being billed for it after the usage period. In these cases, a customer who has four users or processes eight thousand invoices pays for it. This setup is more unpredictable for both customers and the company, but may be perceived as fairer by customers because they will only pay for their actual usage.

A mixture of a license-based and a pay-as-you-go model is a credit-based model. In a credit-based model, customers buy credits that are charged upfront. But the customer can choose when to use the credits. For example, they can pay for credits of ten thousand invoices per month and use eight thousand one month, leading to two thousand invoices carried over to the next month. The benefit of this module is that customers can use what they have paid for whenever they want. Additionally, a credit model can allow multiple features with different price metrics to be combined and sold under one credit metric. This is good if a customer doesn't really know when to consume the credits or what to spend the credits on. The drawback, however, is the model is a bit more complex to explain and sell.

GRANULARITY

The next component to consider in a price model is granularity, i.e., the number of units a customer purchases for a given metric. You can either sell the exact number of units (e.g., 1 or 2.5 units) or sell a tier of volume (e.g., up to five or up to ten units). When selling tiers, customers pay a fixed fee for the tier, regardless of how many units they use within that tier. For example, a customer paying for up to ten units could use three or eight units and still pay the same price. Tiered models are useful for providing buyers with predictable costs and flexibility, as they allow for usage variations without price changes.

Tiers can be uniform (e.g., groups of five) or increasing (e.g., ten to fifteen, sixteen to twenty-five, etc.), depending on the difference between your largest and smallest customers in terms of the metric you apply. For example, the AP automation provider had customers ranging from thousands to millions of invoices per year, which led them to using increasing tiers. Tier sizes should balance the convenience for customers to predict what they will pay, although their volume varies, versus not feeling they pay for more than they need. As a rule of thumb, no tiers are needed if the largest customer is only about ten times larger than the smallest. Uniform tiers work better when the difference is about one hundred times, while increasing tier sizes are more appropriate when the difference approaches one thousand times. If you already have several customers, analyzing their usage or purchase volumes can help define appropriate tier sizes and limits.

A key consideration for tiers is the measurement period, typically monthly or annual. While other periods are possible, they are harder to sell. As a guideline, annual periods are usually better for license-based models, while monthly periods work well for pay-as-you-go or credit-based models.

STRUCTURE

The last price model component is about how a metric scales with the number of units. There are several versions, spanning from fully fixed to fully variable structures. To illustrate some examples, common archetypes are shown in Figure 5.4.[40]

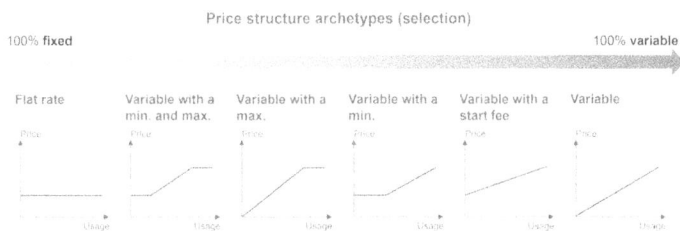

Figure 5.4. Examples of price structures. The examples are linear for illustrative purposes; typically, prices are digressive (i.e., the unit price decreases with the number of units).

The flat fee structure is the most fixed price structure. Every customer pays the same amount regardless of usage. Companies like Spotify use this structure, offering unlimited access to music for a set subscription fee. The advantage of this simplicity is it makes pricing easy for both the provider and the customer to understand and manage. However, it may create perceived inequities: light users may feel they are overpaying, leading to churn, while heavy users receive more value than they pay for.

At the other extreme, the variable fee structure charges customers based entirely on usage, directly aligning costs with consumption. Cloud services like Amazon Web Services use this model, billing customers per gigabyte of data stored or per compute cycle used. While this approach is fairer in terms of value received, it can create cost unpredictability for customers, potentially discouraging usage or leading to budget concerns. To mitigate these issues, many providers adopt a digressive price model, where the unit price decreases as usage increases. This incentivizes customers to use more of the service, supporting long-term ARR growth.

Hybrid price structures blend fixed and variable elements. A common example is a minimum fee combined with usage-based pricing, often used when services include onboarding, basic service levels, or platform access. SaaS platforms may charge a minimum monthly fee that covers core services, with additional charges for extra usage. This structure helps providers cover operational costs and protects against low-commitment customers who may misuse or underutilize the service without contributing adequate revenue.

In some cases, maximum fees are introduced to provide customers with price predictability. This approach is common in pay-as-you-go models, where unexpected spikes in usage could lead to high costs. By capping fees, providers build trust and limit financial risk for customers. However, if not carefully designed, maximum fees can constrain revenue potential, particularly for customers who are willing and able to pay more for high usage. Balancing these trade-offs is crucial to optimizing both customer satisfaction and profitability.

EVALUATING AND SELECTING A PRICE MODEL

To select a price model, begin by creating a comprehensive list of potential options. At this stage, it's beneficial to explore all possibilities, including metrics based on input, process, and outcome, as well as options for modality, granularity, and structure. If your product category already exists, it is useful to look around in the market. Consider whether any price model is the industry standard, what models similar products use, and whether certain price models are more custom to the customers.

Once you have this list, evaluate the price model by considering both customer benefits and benefits to your company. The benefits to customers are often overlooked but are crucial for ensuring the price model is accepted.

It's important to gather direct feedback from customers to understand their perceptions of the model, rather than relying solely on internal assumptions. This input can help align the model with customer needs and expectations.

Here are some typical sub-criteria for what determines the benefits to the customers:[41]

- **Acceptability and fairness:** The pricing should be easy for customers to understand, comparable to competitive offerings, and should scale with perceived value. It should also minimize negative perceptions, such as feeling overcharged due to small hidden fees.
- **Predictability:** A predictable price structure helps customers plan their budgets by offering clarity on the total cost of ownership. This stability ensures that customers can anticipate costs over the long term without surprises.
- **Flexibility:** Customers should have the ability to tailor the scope of services they purchase, allowing them to overcome budget constraints and price thresholds. This adaptability can also encourage incremental upgrades or service expansions over time.

The last factor to consider is the benefits to your company, which includes a subset of criteria, which are typically:

- **Customer adoption:** The price structure should encourage widespread adoption of the product, which in turn facilitates future upsell and cross-sell opportunities by making it easier for customers to explore other offerings in the portfolio.
- **Value capture:** Pricing should scale with customers' future usage and growth. This enables your business to increase prices over time and monetize future product enhancements or add-ons effectively.
- **Ease of implementation:** The price model should be easy for the company to measure, track, and monitor while being straightforward for the sales team to communicate and sell to customers.
- **Tracks with cost:** As the solution scales, the price structure should align with your company's cost structure, ideally ensuring that costs grow proportionally or at a slower rate than revenues. Exploring the cost dynamics is mentioned further in Chapter 6 (Price Level).

The final model is identified by evaluating each price model on the benefit to the customer and to the company, e.g., on a scale from low to high or 1 to 5. The preferred options are those that have both high benefits to your customers and your business. If the benefits are low to your business or your customers, you might suffer either a financial risk to your business or a risk of client attrition. However, the price metrics that bring high value to your customers but low benefit to your business are still suitable for fencing/secondary metrics.

An example of this process is shown in Figure 5.5, which is the assessment for an AP automation solution. However, in the figure, only the metrics are included, but it is possible to include other elements such as modality, granularity, and structure. The preferred option, based on input from customers and from the organization, was to charge based on the number of invoices. Besides invoices, ERPs were used as fencing between products, so customers with more than one ERP couldn't select the most basic package.

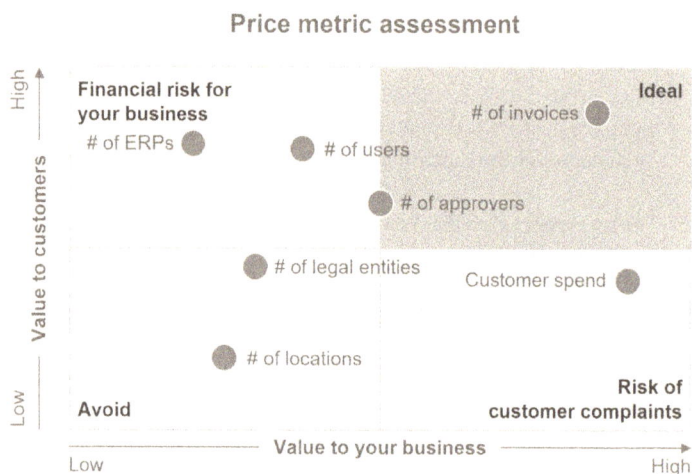

Figure 5.5. Example of evaluating different price metrics.

FAIR USAGE POLICY

In some cases, you may want to use certain price metrics but face obstacles that prevent you from doing so. These obstacles could include having too many price metrics already, making it impractical to add another; the metric being too technical and difficult to explain (e.g., some metrics that limit extreme usage of the product); or the inclusion of a third-party feature with a price model that doesn't align with your own. Despite these challenges, you may still need to manage this metric, especially if excessive usage could lead to significant cost risks.

To address this, you can implement a fair usage policy, which allows customers to use the service up to specified thresholds. This approach enables you to avoid making the restriction a focal point of the sales conversation. However, it's crucial to set the limit high enough so most customers do not reach it. Additionally, you need to define what happens if the threshold is exceeded—whether through a hard stop, performance limitations, or additional fees.

For example, a document management system is initially charged based on users, storage, and the number of objects (e.g., number of files and folders). However, since explaining the number of objects metric proved difficult, it was moved to the fair usage policy in customer contracts.

PRICE MODEL FOR ADD-ONS AND SECONDARY PRODUCTS

When determining the price model, don't forget to consider the price models for other parts of the offering. For example, there might be a different price model for add-ons than for the main product because price models are not necessarily exclusive. It is helpful to think about the overall trade-offs discussed in Chapter 1, particularly the balance between simplicity and complexity (with the potential for additional value capture). Having separate price models for add-ons increases pricing complexity, but this can be justified by higher revenue from additional value capture and less friction in sales.

An example is that an AP automation solution could, for example, charge fees based on the number of invoices for the core product and for certain special integrations, a percentage fee of the payment volume for the payment module, and an hourly fee for any consulting services. Another example is accounting software, where there is typically one metric (e.g., price per user or number of vouchers) for the core accounting service, while there may be other add-ons with different metrics such as price per employee for a salary module, price per invoice for an invoicing module, price per expenses claim for an expense module, price per voucher for accounting support, etc. This ensures that the metric, and in the end the price level, aligns the price paid with the received value.

ALIGN MODEL AND CUSTOMER

Ultimately, your price model should revolve around your customers. Different customers will have different preferences for how they want to be charged, so it's important to factor those preferences in, potentially by tailoring price models to suit different segments.

For example, small customers who are new to your proposition are likely to prefer a pay-as-you-go model or license-/token-based models with small tiers, where they can keep the commitment low and grow over time as they see the value. A large customer, however, who is familiar with your proposition might prefer an unlimited usage model, even if it means a higher price, as they are likely to value cost predictability. Consider each customer segment and their preferences when designing your model.

CONTRACT DURATION AND BILLING FREQUENCY

As part of designing the price model, you should also consider contract duration and billing frequency. Companies typically offer customers varying levels of flexibility, such as different contract durations and billing frequencies. A good rule of thumb is that increased flexibility (e.g., shorter contracts and more frequent billing) should come at a premium.

Standard B2B SaaS contracts are typically rolling agreements with terms of one to three years.[42] For one-year rolling contracts, it's common—especially in enterprise agreements—to include a longer initial commitment period of two or three years. Companies often offer discounts on longer, multi-year contracts to secure customers for extended periods (likewise, companies often apply premiums for shorter contracts). However, if your product has high stickiness and retention, offering discounted long-term deals may lead to unnecessary revenue loss. Longer-term contracts can also be harder to sell and reduce pricing flexibility over time.

For products targeting SMBs or B2C customers, contracts may be month-to-month with cancellation allowed at any time. This level of flexibility should be offered only when necessary, as it can increase churn and reduce revenue predictability.

The other topic is regarding billing frequency. Subscriptions can be offered with various billing frequencies, including annual, monthly, and quarterly options, although annual and monthly are the most common ones.[43] It is normally standard practice to charge a premium for more frequent billing than annual billing, typically around 5–15 percent for quarterly billing and 10–30 percent for monthly billing. The exact premium depends on industry standards, customer preferences, and how you want to incentivize longer-term commitments.

OVERAGES

Overages are charges applied when customers exceed their contracted usage volume, such as their contracted volume of invoices or API calls. Done well, they drive expansion and increased revenue; done poorly, they risk creating confusion and churn. Common approaches include automatic upgrades, where customers are moved to a higher tier after exceeding a limit (however, potential downgrades must be handled manually). While this simplifies billing and promotes growth, it can feel abrupt for customers if not communicated clearly. Another option is pay-as-you-go charges, where customers pay per unit above their limit, often at a premium. This offers customers flexibility but can make costs unpredictable and feel punitive for them. Some companies enforce hard usage caps, blocking access once limits are hit, creating cost control but risking customer disruption.

Oftentimes, the automatic upgrade approach is preferred when it's possible due to driving customers toward larger tiers. However, if the pay-as-you-go method is used, overages should be priced to encourage upgrades without feeling like penalties. But regardless of the model, transparency is essential. Customers should receive alerts when they approach their limits and be informed about their options, giving them time to act before any charges or restrictions apply.

TERMS AND CONDITIONS

The devil is in the details when it comes to the price model. Oftentimes, the terms and conditions are overlooked, which leads to money left on the table. Below are some key areas to keep in mind when setting your terms and conditions. Note that legislation and regulations may differ between markets, in particular if you're selling B2C—ensure, therefore, that you know what to consider in your markets.

- **Basic contract information:** Ensure that the contract auto-renews without triggering renegotiations, and ensure that your company can unilaterally make price changes, product changes, and terms changes. This is to avoid spending unnecessary resources on renegotiations.
- **Define what is negotiable:** Define what terms can be renegotiated (e.g., contract duration and billing frequency) and which ones are not negotiable (e.g., notice period and price increase clause).
- **Price increase clause:** Ensure there is a price increase clause in the contract, and enforce it. There are multiple options, including index-based price increase clauses tied to CPI (or another benchmark) or a fixed percentage price increase.[44] There are also combinations, such as the highest of an index-based clause and a fixed percentage increase, or an index-based uplift plus a fixed percentage price increase. There are often regulations on price increase clauses, especially for B2C, which may vary between markets. Make sure to take these into account.

SUMMARY

- **Select price metric(s):** Modern pricing enables metrics beyond user–input, process, or outcome-based–that better align price with value; choose metrics that reflect usage or results without adding unnecessary complexity.
- **Determine modality, granularity, and structure:** Choose license-based, pay-as-you-go, or credit-based models, then define granularity (exact units or volume tiers) and structure (flat, variable, or hybrid fees). Your selection should balance customer value, pricing predictability, and your ability to capture value.
- **Evaluate price models based on the value to customers and to your business:** To select a price model, explore all viable options, then evaluate each by balancing customer benefits (e.g., fairness, predictability, flexibility) and company benefits (e.g., adoption, monetization, measurability, cost alignment), choosing models that score highly on both.
- **Consider a fair usage clause (if needed):** When a price metric is hard to explain or incompatible with your price model, use fair usage limits in contracts to manage cost risks discreetly. Ensure thresholds are high enough not to impact most customers.
- **Set price models for add-ons and secondary products (if needed):** Add-ons and secondary products may use different price models than the core offering to capture additional value and reduce sales friction.
- **Determine contract duration and billing frequency:** Choose contract lengths and billing intervals based on customer stickiness and industry norms. If possible, price shorter contracts and more frequent billing at a premium to monetize additional flexibility.
- **Review the terms and conditions:** Carefully design your contract terms to support pricing, including auto-renewals, price increase clauses, overage handling, and negotiation limits—while ensuring compliance with local regulations, especially for B2C.

CHAPTER 6

Price Level

DETERMINING FACTORS OF THE PRICE

When you have the architecture set, you can determine price levels. This can be a daunting task, knowing at what point the price is too high (or too low) is tough to predict. It will also depend on all the topics covered so far—from business objectives and customer segmentation, to offering and price model selection—resulting in a particularly complex picture to navigate. But there are several useful methods to use. Before going through the methods, let's review briefly what determines the price.

The factors influencing the price are shown in Figure 6.1.[45] The perceived customer value and competitor prices determine the price ceiling, with more weight put on the more important one. In most cases (except for a pure commodity), the perceived customer value and competitor prices are not the same, but there is a gray zone between them that depends on customers' perceived value of your product and your relative value versus competitors. The company's costs determine the price floor. In addition, business goals and legal constraints (e.g., regulations) can move the price ceiling and price floor in both directions. Note that some of these factors may differ depending on the volume, meaning the willingness to pay or the cost for one unit may differ from those of multiple units.

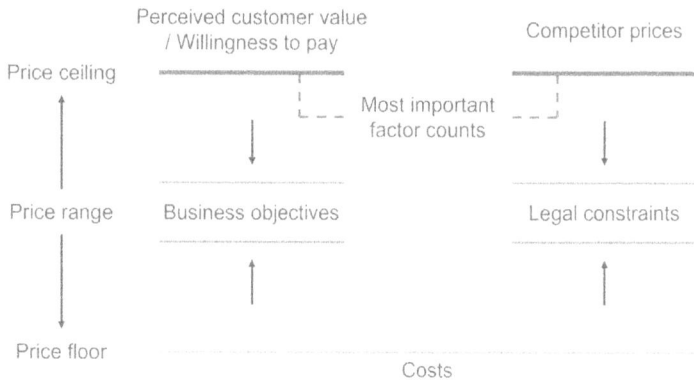

Figure 6.1: Determining factors of the price levels.

Of all the factors that influence the price levels, the perceived customer value/willingness to pay is typically the most difficult part of the picture to figure out. But with the right methods, you can get a decent understanding of it.

SIGNS THAT PRICE INCREASES ARE POSSIBLE

Based on experience, some typical signs indicate that prices can be increased. These include:

- **High customer satisfaction:** High net promoter score (NPS) and customers generally like your product. Furthermore, you get many referrals and recommendations from customers.
- **Low churn:** Churn rate is low, and in case customers leave, price is not the main reason.
- **High win rate:** You often win, and in case you would lose, it's due to other reasons, such as not selecting a solution at all.
- **Few comments about price:** Customers seldom say you're expensive or even say that you're cheap.
- **High customer ROI:** Customers consistently report strong outcomes, such as cost savings, revenue increases, or efficiency gains that far outweigh the price they pay.
- **Significant lock-in:** The cost and/or risk of switching to another solution is high. Alternatively, customers have a high dependency on your product.
- **Large product improvements:** The product has improved significantly in the last years, with new and improved features, but prices have not been increased.

- **Few price adjustments:** Prices have not been increased in several years or even since the product launch.

If you experience some or all of these factors, you should actively think about increasing prices.

CALIBRATING PRICE LEVELS

As mentioned at the beginning of this chapter, several factors impact the prices you can charge. It is important to understand all of these factors to set prices, including a detailed understanding of customer perceptions of your business and the value it provides, how users actually use your products, what key decision-makers in those customer organizations view as successful outcomes, and what the competitive landscape looks like.

In the next subchapters, different methods/analyses for determining price levels are described in more detail. You should aim to use multiple sources to increase the robustness of the results; in particular, customer interviews and surveys should always be conducted. Because these interviews always bring new insights on how customers buy, what they need, and what they are willing to pay, use these insights for setting prices.

However, due to a limited amount of resources, such as limited customer interviews, limited data sets, etc., an extensive method cannot be used for all products. Most likely for the most sold products, you want to really dig into the details, while a pragmatic approach is sufficient for some rare add-ons.

After using the different methods and conducting various analyses, you can summarize your insights and decide how you wish to proceed. When summarizing the data, it is important to look at comparable customers in terms of segment, feature needs (e.g., which package a customer would choose), and volume usage (e.g., number of users or invoices). The outcome can look like Figure 6.2 for the AP automation example. In the figure, there are results for customers with two different volumes in terms of invoices per year but with the same needs in terms of features (basic needs in this example). The dark gray bars show the estimated price interval from each pricing research source. The sources are explained later in this chapter.

Where in the interval you set your price depends on the other factors mentioned in this chapter: the importance of competitors, legal constraints, your business objectives, and costs. For example, if the competition is of low importance and you want to skim the market, you should aim at prices toward the upper end, while if you want to build market share, you likely want to go for the lower end.

Insight from:	10,000 invoices / year			100,000 invoices / year		
	Price per invoice / year (USD)			Price per invoice / year (USD)		
A Economic value	0	1.8–2.7	3	0	1.5–2.3	3
B Van Westendorp (Customer interview)	0	1.8–2.2	3	0	0.5–0.8	3
C Benchmarking (Competitor analysis)	0	1.7–2.3	3	0	0.5–0.9	3
D Van Westendorp (Internal exercise)	0	1.9–2.3	3	0	0.7–0.9	3
Considering strategy	0	1.9–2.0	3	0	0.6–0.7	3

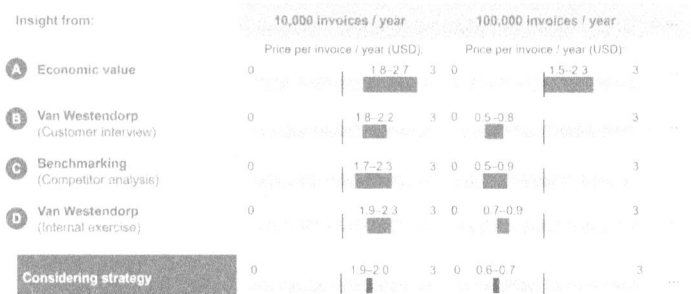

Figure 6.2: Example of a pricing research summary. Costs are also considered besides the listed methods.

When you have determined specific price points, you can then use them to create the price structure. With that price structure, you can calculate all the other prices for that product.

ECONOMIC VALUE

First, you should develop a clear understanding of the economic value or ROI your solution can deliver to the customer. This involves:

- Identifying the key business outcomes your customers are aiming for, such as increased revenue, cost savings, or emotional benefits like peace of mind
- Collaborating with customers to identify the KPIs that your solution improves
- Demonstrating how those improvements directly support their desired business outcomes
- Estimating the share of that economic value your company can reasonably capture through pricing

In some cases, this will be straightforward. For instance, subscription analytics tools like ChartMogul can clearly show revenue impact. Whereas a platform like Skillshare (an online learning service) might find it more difficult to pinpoint the right metrics and demonstrate its influence on outcomes.

Nonetheless, investing time in understanding economic value is worth the effort. It not only helps you define an appropriate price level but also equips your sales and marketing teams to articulate and demonstrate value, both during the buying process and after implementation.

Note, however, you can seldom capture the full savings in the price. Based on their own and others' experience, companies are typically able to charge between 10–30 percent of the economic value created, depending on the price model used.[46]

You can learn much about the economic value by interviewing your customers. The questions seek to understand quantified benefits (such as revenue increase, cost reductions, productivity improvements, and risk reductions) and unquantified benefits (such as increased customer satisfaction and an improved onboarding process). Some questions to consider:

- How do buyers think about the value and ROI of the solution?
- How would they pitch the business case internally?
- How does the buying process work, and what's the threshold for a deal to go to procurement (if relevant)?
- What would be the risks of no longer using the solution?

Another benefit with this research is that these questions are difficult to lowball, as opposed to questions directly asking about the price. However, they are a bit trickier to translate into price points.

SWITCHING COSTS/STICKINESS

Switching costs are both a curse and a blessing. If you're the incumbent provider, these costs work in your favor. They reduce the risk of churn and give you more flexibility to raise prices. But if you're trying to win over a customer from a competitor with high switching barriers, you'll likely need to start with a more aggressive pricing strategy to win the deal and grow the account later.

Nevertheless, you should evaluate the cost of switching both from a competitor's product to yours and from your product to a competitor's. Some key considerations include data migration costs, such as the time and effort required to transfer and validate data, and integration costs for connecting the new SaaS product with existing systems and workflows. Training and onboarding costs may also arise as employees adapt to the new platform. Additionally, there is the risk of losing customizations or features if the new solution cannot replicate specific configurations. Transitioning can disrupt business operations, affecting productivity and service delivery. Finally, change management efforts are required to address internal resistance and align stakeholders with the new system. These costs make switching less appealing and reduce the likelihood of customers moving to competitors.

ALTERNATIVES/COMPETITORS

As mentioned above, the price or cost of alternatives is a fundamental input when determining your pricing. Key sources to consider include:

- **Competitor pricing:** Identify all relevant competitors and gather information on their pricing. There may be multiple similar offerings to evaluate.
- **Cost of inaction:** Many customers stick with outdated or manual processes simply because they are familiar. Estimate the cost of doing nothing as a baseline comparison.
- **Cost of indirect or nontraditional alternatives:** Look beyond direct competitors and consider substitute solutions outside your typical competitive set. Estimate the price of these alternatives to fully understand your pricing context.

In many cases, particularly for businesses targeting SMBs, pricing is available on competitors' websites, and discounting is relatively limited. In contrast, for larger deals, pricing is often less transparent, and discounting is more common, making it harder to benchmark competitive pricing accurately. However, you can gain insights through competitor product demos or mystery shopping (i.e., pretending to be a normal customer when you are employed by a company to check how competitor products are being sold).

When comparing prices, the key is to try to get a "like for like" comparison, which means you must verify what features and benefits are included in the product you compare with. Furthermore, you should consider the total cost of ownership over a set of years to account for the fact that some competitors may charge for certain features and benefits separately instead of having them included in the main fee.

Price comparisons become more complex when dealing with credit- or token-based models, which require translating usage into actual costs. Additionally, consider differences in performance across other key buying criteria, such as reliability, support quality, and brand reputation, which can significantly impact perceived value.

Finally, consider switching costs, which can pose a significant barrier for customers considering a change in solution.

COST DYNAMICS

The price floor is defined by your costs. It's important to understand how these costs scale across customers based on the scope of their purchases, how they use your product, and the level of service provided. In this analysis, consider both direct costs, such as those incurred when adding a new customer, and fixed costs. Common cost drivers include customer acquisition (sales and marketing), hosting, support, and any bundled service components. For offerings that include direct costs, such as dedicated consultant hours or hardware, these must also be factored in. For more on this topic, see Chapter 9 (Special Topics).

COMMERCIAL DATA

If you have several customers already, you can analyze historical data to understand the willingness to pay. Data of interest is normally current contractual data, win/loss reasons, and churn reasons. In addition, you want to use any available customer segmentation information to study if there is any pattern regarding what prices certain customer segments have accepted (and not) and what the key reasons for churn are. Some example analyses are:

- **Price spreads:** Look at the price spread for comparable products and review what the twentieth or eightieth percentiles of prices are. Then compare those numbers between segments and get an understanding of what describes customers with relatively high and low prices.
- **Win/loss:** Analyze the sales funnel and study conversion rates between the funnel stages to review if and how pricing explains the conversion rates. For won deals, analyze what discounts were granted (and why) and how those vary between segments.
- **Churn data:** Review the churn reasons for different segments. Analyze if there is any particular segment churning, if there are any particular churn reasons, and if price is a key reason.

You may, for example, find that customers with certain characteristics tend to pay higher prices; this type of insight can then be systematized and exploited. Analyzing commercial data, especially win/loss reasons, can reveal what top-performing salespeople do differently, such as consistently winning more deals at better prices. These insights can then be applied systematically to improve outcomes across the entire sales team, for example, through additional segment- and deal-specific price guidance.

USAGE DATA

Understanding how customers use your product is essential for identifying which aspects are most valuable and to whom. For instance, a company that relies on your product daily is likely willing to pay more than one that uses it only once a week. Similarly, customers leveraging advanced functionalities are likely to perceive greater value and be willing to pay more than those using only basic features.

While usage analytics won't provide the exact "right price" to charge, they can help you identify customer segments deriving the most value from your product. This insight allows you to establish differentiated price levels or implement price increases based on customer engagement and traction. To maximize these insights, combine usage analytics with data on what customers are paying to develop data-driven insights into the relationship between usage and willingness to pay.

CUSTOMER INTERVIEWS

Interviewing customers provides insights into what they value and how much they are willing to pay. However, direct questions such as "how much would you like to pay?" tend not to bring meaningful outcomes because respondents may answer lower than what their actual willingness to pay is. Common methodologies for asking about the price are the van Westendorp technique, Gabor-Granger approach, and conjoint analysis.

The van Westendorp technique can be done with a relatively small sample size; the data can come from one-on-one conversations or an online survey of buyers.[47] The idea of the methodology is that you ask the following questions:

- At what price would you consider the product to be so expensive that you would not consider buying it? (Too expensive)
- At what price would you consider the product to be priced so low that you would feel the quality couldn't be very good? (Too cheap)
- At what price would you consider the product starting to get expensive so that it is not out of the question, but you would have to give some thought to buying it? (Expensive)
- At what price would you consider the product to be a bargain—a great buy for the money? (Cheap)

Due to the van Westendorp easily becoming repetitive, an idea could be to ask two of the questions instead of four, but for more than one product. When asking these questions, you need to be specific about what is included so that you can analyze the results without any biases. In the case of the AP automation product, screening questions were asked to understand the needs in terms of features and invoice volume, to then ask them the van Westendorp questions for a package including those features and volumes. Furthermore, specify how the customer should answer, in case they want to respond as a price per invoice or a total annual or monthly price.

In Figure 6, the responses from customers with ten thousand invoices per year are displayed. As you can see, the responses are displayed as the accumulated share of respondents at each price threshold, with the "Cheap" and "Too Cheap" being decreasing sums, while "Expensive" and "Too Expensive" are increasing sums. From the output, you can find the acceptable price range, which is from the intercept between "Too cheap" and "Expensive" to the intercept between "Cheap" and "Too expensive." In this case, the acceptable price range is 1.8 to 2.2 USD per invoice. Furthermore, you can also identify "price thresholds," which are price points where the demand drops significantly. In Figure 6.3, the price points 1.5, 2, and 2.5 USD are some examples.

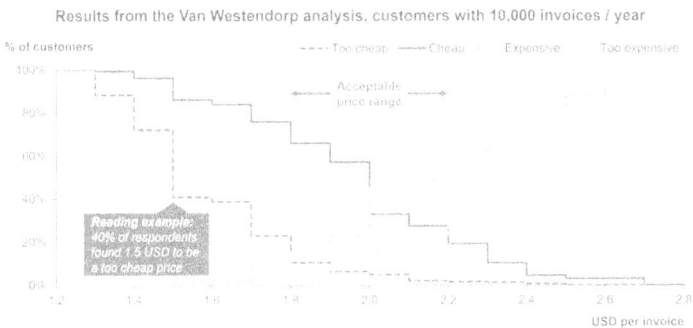

Figure 6.3: The results from the van Westendorp questions for customers with ten thousand invoices per year.

Another common method is the Gabor-Granger approach,[48] which asks customers how willing they are to buy at different price points. Respondents may be asked to answer either "Yes, I would buy" or "No, I wouldn't buy," or to rate their likelihood on a scale from one to five, where one means "Definitely would not buy" and five means "Definitely would buy." By testing multiple price points, one identifies the highest price at which the customer is still willing to buy, which can then be translated into a demand curve.

To use the Gabor-Granger method in a survey or an interview, you must find the highest price that respondents are willing to pay. There are many ways to do this, but the most common is usually done by choosing several price points (usually five through seven, but it could be any number as long as it's manageable), and then asking the respondent if they would buy the product for a random price from those established price points. If the respondent answers yes to this question, they are then asked the same question for a random price that is higher than the one just asked. If it is a no, then the respondent is asked the same question for a random lower price. This is done until you find the highest price the respondent answers yes to. The results are then summarized by analyzing how many would buy at each price point, from which it's possible to calculate profit and revenue-maximizing prices.

A third method is a conjoint analysis. Conjoint analysis is a statistical technique used in market research to understand customer preferences and decision-making by evaluating how people value different features of a product or service.[49] It involves presenting respondents with a series of product or service profiles that vary in attributes and asking them to choose or rank their preferences. The method helps identify the relative importance of each attribute (e.g., price, quality, features) and how changes in these affect customer choices. Conjoint methods are a bit more complex and require a larger sample size, and are therefore, based on my experience, less frequently used in pricing surveys/interviews.

For some of the noncore features and services, there are simpler, but still useful, questions to use. In those scenarios, it could be sufficient to just ask about the relative value between different products or packages. For example, asking how much more the customer would be willing to pay for a solution with premium support than without it, all other things being equal. These questions could also be asked as simplified versions of the van Westendorp, such as what acceptable and expensive value differences would be.

SALES TEAM AND PARTNER EXERCISES

If you or your sales partners have closed many deals already, a source could be to ask your sales team or your sales partners about price levels. The sales team and the partners are, after all, the people who are closest to the market and should have an understanding of what acceptable price levels are. You could ask them price questions, such as van Westendorp, or you could ask them to estimate which price levels they would quote for different win rates, e.g., what price level would lead to a 20 percent and 50 percent win rate. These exercises could bring insights into the sales team's and the partners' views on achievable prices. These exercises also unveil differences between the respondents, which could be useful to understand why (and how) certain respondents believe a higher price is more achievable than others.

EXPERIMENT WITH PRICE LEVELS

If your aim is rather to fine-tune prices, practical experiments are also an option. To begin with, if you have many customers or website visitors, A/B testing can help identify what works best. An A/B test is, in brief, a test where you, for example, present the offering model and price levels in different ways for two different populations to study which way performs the best on certain predefined success criteria. Another approach is to gradually test different offering models or price levels and monitor their performance. The key for all experiments is to ensure you have a sufficient sample size to draw meaningful conclusions, clearly define success criteria before the experiment, and establish a plan for how to proceed if the experiments do not yield the desired outcomes.

BUSINESS OBJECTIVES AND ITEM ROLES

Price levels are fundamentally a reflection of your company's strategy and business objectives. Various factors, including product maturity, the role of each item in your portfolio, and your focus on growth versus profitability, all shape how prices should be set. By aligning price levels with these goals, you can better support your long-term commercial strategy.

Products often play different roles within a portfolio. Some may serve as growth drivers designed to attract new customers, even at a low or negative margin. This approach, commonly used by supermarkets with loss leaders, works by creating a clear path for upselling more profitable offerings. For instance, in SaaS businesses, a core product might be priced competitively to drive adoption, with the expectation that users will later purchase high-margin add-ons or upgrades.

Conversely, certain products or services may have low price sensitivity, allowing you to charge premium prices and maximize profitability. A common example is professional services offered alongside a SaaS product. These services, such as consulting or custom integrations, may not be a priority for customers at the time of initial purchase but become essential later, enabling higher margins. Similarly, add-ons can often be priced for profitability rather than wide adoption, as they cater to a smaller but high-value segment of customers.

Ultimately, your pricing should reflect both the role of each product in your portfolio and your broader business objectives. Revisiting your monetization strategy, as outlined in Chapter 1, is crucial when setting price levels. By strategically balancing growth and profitability through item roles and tailored pricing, you can strengthen both customer acquisition and long-term revenue potential.

HOW TO SET COMPLETELY NEW PRICES

Your price-setting approach depends foremost on two factors: to what extent it is a new category and how many deals you can close in a year. The number of deals you can close per year determines how fast you can start sampling commercial and usage data to analyze, and is driven by the price of your product, the number of customers, and the sales cycle length. The pricing methods to consider are summarized in Figure 6.4.

In all cases, you should conduct an economic value analysis and conduct customer interviews. These analyses are particularly important if you have only a few deals per year because it will take time to get sufficient data from the deals themselves.

If you have many deals per year, you will quite rapidly get data on both commercial performance (win/loss, discounts, other feedback, etc.) and usage, which will help you refine the packaging and pricing. Furthermore, when you have many deals per year, you can A/B test different concepts much more easily, due to getting rapid responses and lower stakes. Sampling, analyzing, and testing of data is still possible when you make a few deals per year, but the process needs to be more qualitative and carefully planned.

In the case of the product being in an existing category, you will also have the advantage of analyzing competitors and alternatives. In these cases, you can find experts with insights into the value delivered and corresponding prices of the competitors/alternatives, and/or you can conduct mystery shopping to understand their packaging and pricing. There are cases where a new category can have alternatives, although not fully comparable, and then you should consider these alternatives if relevant.

Over time, you can gather data on commercial performance and product usage, regardless of whether the product category is new or established, or whether you close many deals annually or only a few. This information is invaluable for refining your offering and pricing strategies, as the perceived value of a product can change significantly over time.

Kyle Poyar's findings[50] for SaaS companies highlight this evolution throughout venture capital investment rounds. From the Seed to Expansion investment rounds, prices can increase by approximately 60 percent due to a clearer ICP and stronger product-market fit. During the Expansion to Growth investment rounds, prices may rise by another 40 percent, driven by additional proof points and growing confidence in the product. Finally, between the Growth investment round and Exit/IPO, prices can see a further 20 percent increase as companies offer more products and cater to larger customers. These insights demonstrate the substantial potential of actively optimizing pricing throughout a product's lifecycle.

Figure 6.4: Price-setting methods based on product type.

PRICE DIFFERENTIATION (INCLUDING INTERNATIONAL PRICING)

Different customer segments may exhibit varying willingness to pay, even when they use the product in the same way. Common differentiators include geography, industry, or other segment-specific factors. To address these differences, price differentiation can be implemented by setting distinct price levels for the same product and usage combination. However, this approach is only worthwhile if the differences in willingness to pay between segments are substantial enough to justify the added complexity. Otherwise, the extra effort may not deliver sufficient value. This ties back to your overall pricing strategy and the trade-off between maintaining simplicity and optimizing for segment-specific willingness to pay.

There are two primary approaches to price differentiation: differentiating list prices or applying different discounts. The key distinction lies in transparency—list price differentiation is typically more visible to customers, while discounts can be less apparent. The decision to differentiate pricing depends on the level of transparency your business is willing to embrace and which channel strategy you have (e.g., list price differentiation is the only option for self-service).

Furthermore, due to the relatively high transparency of list prices, consider these two factors before implementing list price differentiation:

1. **An efficient fencing is possible:** Ensure it is possible customers can buy at their price level. For example, if you differentiate prices by country, ensure that customers cannot purchase the product from a lower-priced region.
2. **There is an acceptance:** Evaluate whether customers will accept the price differences. If not well justified, price variations, such as displaying different prices on your website for identical products offered to different segments, may lead to a negative impact on conversion rates, customer satisfaction, and retention.

In case fencing is not possible and the acceptance is lacking, it is more favorable to differentiate the discounts instead. Discounts are explained in the next subchapter.

DISCOUNTS

For products sold through direct or indirect sales channels, discounts are often a key part of the sales process.

Here are typical steps for determining discounts:

- **Set a maximum discount level based on, e.g.:**
  - Average discount of current customers
  - Lower end willingness to pay from market research
  - Competitor benchmarking
  - Minimum profitability
- **Split the maximum discount level into fixed and variable components:**
  - For instance, a baseline of 10 percent by default is allowed for every customer, without taking discount drivers into account.
  - The rest of the discount is variable based on discount drivers.
- **The variable discount is based on discount drivers (e.g., market/customer/deal specifics):**
  - Each discount driver contributes to a certain extent to the total discount that can be granted to a customer.

To get input on the maximum discount, an idea is to ask customers about discount expectations. Some procurement departments may have KPIs related to the discounts, which interviews could unveil as well. However, the list price should not be extremely different from the net price. The list price serves as a signal for the value of the product and should not be outlandishly high, or customers will grow fatigued.

For the variable part, these are typically based on different drivers, which are customer dimensions correlating well with willingness to pay. These are specific to your company and product, but there are, however, several categories that can frequently be leveraged effectively:

- **Customer location:** Where customers are located can have a large impact on willingness to pay, due to differences in purchasing power across economies, differences in local competitive intensity, and the availability of regional alternatives.
- **Customer industry/sector:** Product-market fit and use case can often vary by industry, as well as the underlying profitability of the industry itself.
- **Customer size:** In most cases, the price metric will scale naturally with customer size; however, if that is not the case, there may be a difference in willingness to pay based on size metrics, such as revenue, number of employees, etc.
- **Deal specifics:** In large or complex negotiations, price can often serve as a strategic lever to influence the outcome of a deal. Variations in the balance of power and competitive intensity across different negotiations create opportunities to optimize win rates by adjusting pricing strategically.

By analyzing differences in willingness to pay between segments, you can put together discount guidelines similar to those in Figure 6.5., where price reductions (or increases) depend on the customer's specifics. This helps the salesperson know what an acceptable price is in each situation.

Example of discount guidelines for an AP automation company

Base discount (Allowed for all deals)	10%			
Volume discount (Based on customer ARR)	0%	4%	8%	12%
Industry discount (Based on the industry)	0%	4%	0%	
Market discount (Based on the market)	0%	4%	0%	
Complexity discount (Based on AP complexity)	-3%	0%	3%	
Maximum discount (Sum of all factors)	19%	Highlighted boxes indicate relevant criteria in this example		

Figure 6.5: Example of discount guidelines. Note that a negative discount means a premium/lower discount.

In addition, you should consider the discount mandate, if a salesperson has the authority to discount fully based on the guidelines, or if there should be any escalation to a sales manager or a deal desk. More information about delegation of authority and escalation is in Chapter 7 (Price Communication).

Last, a word of caution: it's important to balance the simplicity of your pricing guidance with the opportunity to optimize prices. Just because price differentiation is possible and may increase revenue doesn't mean it's the right move. As businesses become more global and centralize procurement, inconsistent or hard-to-justify price variations can create confusion, slow down the sales process, or shut you out completely.

DISCOUNT TACTICS TO CONSIDER

For some reason, discounts are often given at levels of 5 or 10 percent. A fairly quick way of increasing margins is to discount less, such as steps of 4 or 7 percent. Oftentimes, it's not about the percentage amounts per se; it's about the gesture of giving something.

Furthermore, when discounting, avoid price discounts that are more or less permanent. Oftentimes, customers get used to the discounted price levels and resist paying higher subscription fees at a later stage. As an alternative, rather give time-limited discounts, such as two months for free or a 20 percent discount during the first year. In addition, try to give discounts in the form of nonmonetary benefits rather than in price. This could be additional add-ons, volume, users, or access to a more premium package for a limited time. Another option is to discount any potential onboarding fee rather than the recurring fee.

As a last resort, use price discounts, but ensure you have mechanisms in place to increase prices in the future, such as a price increase clause in the contract and a routine of monitoring and addressing discounts. Consider using tools such as a CRM or subscription management system to manage discounts and avoid unnecessary leakage.

Finally, when discounting, salespeople should also ask for something in return. Examples could be to ask customers to buy more volume, a more premium offering, or buy more add-ons in exchange for additional discounts.

SUMMARY

- **Use the most suitable price-setting methods (ideally multiple methods):** Set price levels by combining multiple data sources—customer interviews, value analysis, competitor pricing, internal cost data, and usage insights. Focus deeper research on core products, align price decisions with business goals, and validate the price levels through testing and feedback, where possible.
- **Consider price differentiation (both on a list price and discount level):** Use price differentiation when segments show significantly different willingness to pay, but only if the added complexity is justified; prefer discount differentiation over list price differentiation when customer acceptance is low or fencing between segments is difficult.
- **Develop discount guidelines (considering both amount and type):** Establish clear discount guidelines based on customer willingness to pay and deal specifics. Limit unnecessary discounting, prefer time-limited or nonmonetary discounts, ensure mechanisms are in place to recover margin over time, and encourage sales teams to seek something in return when they provide discounts.

CHAPTER 7

Price Communication

SETTING A PRICE IS NOT ENOUGH

After setting the prices, the next steps are to defend/enforce them. To charge your desired price levels based on the value you deliver, you also need to communicate this value to your customers. Hence, you need to ensure the appropriate sales and marketing material is in place. This chapter covers some of these aspects that are often covered in combination with packaging and pricing design projects. Note, however, there are plenty of books and guides on sales in case you want to learn more.[51]

OFFERINGS AND PRICES ON THE WEB PAGE

If and how you present your prices on the web page depends on several factors, among others, your channel strategy. If you offer self-service, you need information online. If you sell via your own sales team or partners, you don't need to put prices online, although it might still be a good idea. There are several pros and cons of having prices on the website to consider.

The pros of pricing on your website are the transparency to the customers, which may build trust, boost conversion, and increase enquiries. The cons, on the other hand, include showing your price to competitors. This might lead to missed opportunities from customers who think the prices on the website are too high, and it may lead to less engagement due to less interaction with the sales team. Hence, you should likely list pricing on your website if you sell products and want customers to buy online. The bottom line is the majority of customers still prefer to see some form of pricing before deciding to buy or contact a business for more information. But if it is challenging to give a good estimation online, and if you want to interact with the customer in connection with price, you should not list it.

Regardless of whether you show prices or not, you should still leverage your website to display your offering and describe the value your offering delivers so customers know what you have to offer before reaching out. The pricing page is normally one of the most visited sites on your webpage. You want to ensure that prospective customers can find information about your products and their value on the site. There is a lot of advice on how to design a pricing page.[52]

Here are considerations based on experience:

- The number of price plans. Do not have too many plans; more than four is uncommon.
- The length of feature lists. Avoid lengthy lists of features, display only the most important ones, or display features in a way to make it less lengthy.
- Presentation of prices (in case you decide to display them). Use some of the behavioral pricing concepts (see next subchapter) and ensure customers can easily get prices in their preferred currency.
- Presentation of plans. Highlight a preferred option to facilitate customers who are indecisive in making a selection.
- Elaborating plan titles. If your offering allows it, consider a more descriptive naming convention and use a microcopy/description of the target customer.
- A call-to-action button. Make it eye-catching and clear, and use an engaging title, such as "Get Started," "Try for Free," or "Contact Sales."

In addition, remember some basic items to consider:

- User interface. Ensure the page is easy to interact with, the basic information is presented in a structured way, and it is visually appealing.
- Customer support. Offer live chat and answers to frequently asked questions on the website to help customers who have questions.
- Value reminders. Include value proposition, supplementary messages, and customer testimonials on the site.

Remember to continuously refine your pricing page. You can test different adjustments to see what drives the most engagement, either as purchases on the website or customers reaching out for more information.

BEHAVIORAL PRICING

The psychological aspects of price have attracted considerable attention in recent years, beyond the economic and quantitative profit effects. When presenting your offering and prices, keep psychological concepts in mind due to the large impact they can have on profits. These concepts are based on the fact that people take shortcuts when making decisions and may appear irrational.[53] But leveraging them facilitates nudging customers in your desired direction. All details are not listed here, but here are some main concepts to consider:[54]

- **Anchor price effects:** Customers judge the value of a product relative to the first price they see, not just on absolute value. Showing a 299 USD Enterprise plan first makes the 99 USD Pro plan feel like a bargain, even if the customer never intended to buy Enterprise.
- **The magic of the middle:** When given three options, many customers choose the middle one by default, assuming it's the safest bet., such as offering Basic (49 USD), Pro (99 USD), and Enterprise (199 USD). Most customers gravitate to Pro, especially if it's designed to match common needs.
- **Expanding a price range:** Introducing a higher-priced option shifts the perceived value of existing plans upward. Adding a 499 USD "Platinum" plan can boost conversions for the 199 USD Enterprise plan, even if few choose Platinum.
- **Default options:** Highlighting a particular plan as "Recommended" or "Most Popular" nudges customers toward that option. Marking the 99 USD Pro plan as "Best Value" leads more users to select it, assuming it offers the best trade-off.
- **Paradox of choice:** Too many options can overwhelm users and reduce conversion. Simpler choices lead to faster decisions. Limiting your offering to three to four pricing tiers avoids confusion and improves sign-up rates compared to showing six to seven plans.
- **Creating scarcity:** Perceived scarcity drives urgency and increases perceived value. For example, "Only five onboarding slots left this month" encourages faster decision-making and reduces sales cycles.
- **Decoy effect:** A deliberately less attractive option can make the target plan seem like a much better deal. E.g., including a 189 USD plan with fewer features than the 199 USD plan makes the latter feel like a no-brainer.
- **Price as an indicator of quality:** Especially in uncertain markets, higher prices are assumed to reflect better quality or more reliable service. For example, a 149 USD analytics tool is perceived as more robust and enterprise-ready than a 49 USD alternative, even before a trial.

The revenue effects that come from the application of these insights into price psychology are often significant. But a word of caution is not to abuse them because that may lead to customers feeling cheated and thereby reacting very negatively.

PRICE THRESHOLDS

Price thresholds are defined as certain prices that, when exceeded, result in a sharp drop in sales. Such price thresholds are normally round numbers such as one, five, ten, or one hundred. Many prices end just below this, very often at the number nine.

The main argument for the existence of odd prices is that customers perceive the digits in a price with decreasing intensity as they often read from left to right. The first digit in a price has the strongest influence on perception, i.e., a price of 4.99 USD comes across as 4 USD plus something rather than 5 USD. Neuropsychologists have confirmed that the further to the right a digit is, the less influence it has on price perception. According to this hypothesis, customers underestimate prices that lie just under round numbers.

The belief that price thresholds exist has led to the widespread practice of using odd prices, which are prices not ending in zero. When customers grow accustomed to these odd prices, they can show heightened sensitivity to prices and price increases that breach nearby thresholds. Despite the frequency of reported cases such as these, convincing scientific evidence for a general price-threshold effect is still lacking.[55] What we typically see, however, is that price thresholds are normally considered in self-service sales while seldom being considered in sales-led sales.

SALES MATERIAL

If you sell the product through your sales team, it is key for them to sell based on value rather than on price. To enable this, a good idea is to compile a "sales playbook" that includes the material they need to convince the customer of the value of the product. These are things to have in place for efficient price communication:

- **Value driver list and analysis:** Understand what drives value among the customers, based on assessment of your own and competitors' offerings.
- **Product and service offering:** Summary of the products and services to offer each customer segment.

- **Sales material and presentations:** Sales materials, presentations, and product descriptions adapted to targeted segments.
- **Value-selling arguments:** Key benefits and value arguments adapted for each customer segment.
- **Counterarguments and questions:** Arguments and questions to use in response to objections.
- **Negotiation best practice:** Collection of best practices when negotiating in terms of preparation, execution, and follow-up.
- **Allowed concessions:** Rules for giving discounts and what to ask in return, counterarguments.
- **Sales-training material:** Collection of sales material and best practices used in training and as reference material.

Based on experience, it is rare these materials are in place, even in large multinational companies. And even if they are in place, they are not maintained frequently enough to make them up-to-date and useful in practice.

When writing value-selling arguments, the focus must be on the customers, their daily workflows, and their pain points. Customers care about how a product can make their lives easier or solve challenges they have. The features that help deliver those outcomes are only a means to an end and not what customers are ultimately interested in. Simply put: customers don't buy features. They buy the benefits the features bring them.

A good value-selling argument is based on a positioning statement, supported with the benefits related to the statement, and then backed up with "reasons to believe," or "proof-points," such as market studies, case studies, or other proof. An example of the AP automation solution is shown in Figure 7.1, where the main positioning statement is about the peace of mind and control the solution brings, and the supporting statements are benefits related to this general statement. For each supporting statement, there are reasons to believe in the form of data and case studies. These parameters, such as an 80 percent time saving, can then quantify the impact in monetary terms, for example, by calculating savings based on invoice volume and processing time.

Paddle Studios, a data-driven revenue automation and optimization platform, has demonstrated through its research that positioning statements can have as much as a 40 percent impact on a customer's perceived willingness to pay for B2B propositions.[56] Having a full customer case study demonstrating the value of the proposition can increase willingness to pay by 20 percent. These insights underline just how important positioning and messaging are for influencing a customer's perception of value and price.

Positioning statement	Benefits	Reasons to believe / Proof-points (Based on feedback from customers)
	Import invoices effortlessly Eliminate manual data entry and streamline your workflow with rapid invoice import options.	• 80% time-savings in data entry by automating invoice import processes, eliminating manual input errors, and reducing processing time. • 95% reduction in data entry errors, ensuring greater accuracy in financial records.
Less Stress. More Control. Smarter AP.	Accelerate approvals. Speed up your invoice approval process with digital, automated workflows— approve with a single click, instantly.	• 90% reduction in manual approval intervention, freeing up staff time and improving overall workflow efficiency. • 30% improvement in compliance by ensuring standardized and consistent approval processes.
	Unlock business insights Leverage powerful analytics and reporting to optimize payment timing, analyze expenses, and improve cash flow—all based on real-time data.	• 20% improvement in payment timing by analyzing and optimizing cash flow and payment schedules. • 25% reduction in late payments by identifying trends in real-time. • 10–15% reduction in operational costs through improved financial forecasting and decision-making based on accurate data.

Figure 7.1. Describe the benefits related to each feature and back up the benefits with data.

In addition to the value-selling arguments, you also need to prepare for potential objections or counterquestions. Frequent objections are related to price ("you're too expensive") or functionalities ("your competitor is better"). Below are some key considerations for handling objections:

- **Listen and empathize:** Fully hear the prospect's objection without interrupting, and acknowledge their concern. This builds rapport and shows you care about their perspective.
- **Clarify:** Ask follow-up questions to ensure you understand the exact issue. Clarification helps you address the real concern, not just what they initially mentioned.
- **Address and provide value:** Respond with a solution that highlights benefits, features, or proof (e.g., testimonials or data). Focus on how your product solves their problem or adds value.
- **Confirm:** Ask if your response has resolved the concern (e.g., "Does that address your issue?"). This ensures you've fully addressed their objection before moving forward.
- **Stay positive:** Maintain a professional, calm, and solution-focused attitude. A positive demeanor reassures the prospect and keeps the conversation constructive.

The key to handling objections is similar to that for other sales elements: preparation. It is possible to prepare by thinking through common objections and collecting internal best practices on how to counter them.

Chapter 2 (Customer Segmentation) discussed the importance-performance matrix for certain buying criteria. This analysis could also be used for preparing value-selling arguments, as shown in Figure 7.2. The competitive advantages are the main talking points and are the criteria you should focus on in your sales process. For the competitive disadvantages, you should prepare counterarguments, and you can generalize the low performance to be an industry-wide problem. For the overperformance ones, prepare arguments that explain your strengths and try to make those criteria appear more important than they are. The low-importance ones should likely not be mentioned by your customers or by yourself, but prepare counterarguments for those points as well if needed.

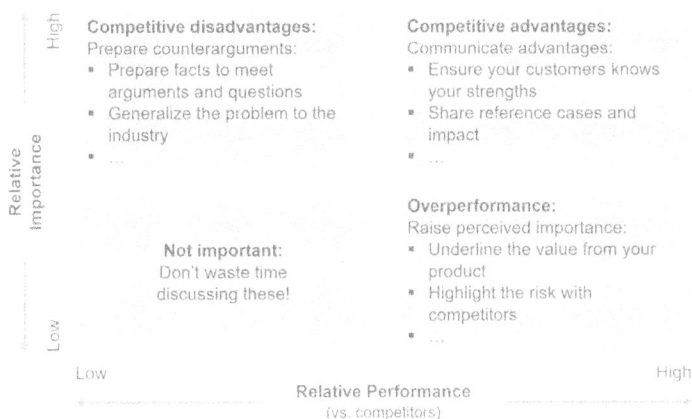

Figure 7.2: How to use the importance-performance matrix for value argumentation.

DELEGATION OF AUTHORITY

This book has repeatedly stressed the importance of understanding customer needs and customer's willingness to pay. But being customer-centric doesn't mean saying yes to every request or customizing everything to fit individual demands. You need clear guidelines around what your teams are allowed—and not allowed—to do for customers. That way, sales, customer success, and other frontline teams know their limits and can act with confidence.

There's no one-size-fits-all approach, but a good delegation of authority should cover a few key areas:

- **Packaging:** Set rules on whether (and when) the packaging can be adjusted for a specific customer. As a general rule, avoid selling nonstandard packages—it adds complexity and drives up your cost to serve. Still, there might be exceptions for large or strategic accounts. Whatever policy you choose, make sure it's well-documented and communicated clearly.

- **Price discounts:** Be clear on how much the discount is (in dollars or percentage) your team members can offer, and in which situations. You might need different rules depending on the sales channel or product. In enterprise deals, some discount flexibility is typically expected, while for smaller accounts, a simplified and more restrictive discount policy is generally better for protecting your margins.
- **Terms and conditions adjustments:** Determine what deviations in the terms and conditions are allowed and what are not. Typically, you do not want to allow any flexibility regarding, for example, notice periods and price increase clauses, while you may allow deviations in contract duration and billing frequency, such as allowing monthly billing instead of annual billing.

Related to the delegation of authority, it is key to think through what escalation levels there should be and who the approver should be. Normally, salespeople should have some kind of negotiation room to close deals relatively independently, while larger discounts, tailored packaging, and special terms and conditions require further approval.

Some companies have a deal desk to help sales teams handle complex deals and make sure policies are followed. This can offer advantages, like more consistent quoting, but be careful it doesn't create unnecessary delays.

SALES INCENTIVES

When setting prices, it's important to align the incentive model with your strategy to promote productive behaviors in customer-facing teams. Misaligned incentives can result in issues such as excessive discounting or misplaced priorities. Start by ensuring your business objectives, monetization model, and incentives are fully aligned, particularly regarding the balance between growth and profitability. Communicate how incentives support pricing goals to foster ownership and accountability. Transparency helps teams understand how their actions contribute to overall success.

Teams should have visibility into how incentives are structured and the ability to influence key factors. It's also important to understand what motivates your team, including the balance between variable and fixed components. Remember that monetary rewards are not the only drivers of performance—nonmonetary incentives, such as recognition and awards, can also be highly effective.

A common challenge is when incentives are overly focused on growth or ARR, with insufficient attention to price realization. This can lead to excessive discounting to close deals. To address this, establish clear escalation paths to control discounting. Alternatively, incorporate a margin-based component to encourage sales teams to protect profitability by limiting discounts.

In organizations with multiple sales roles, such as field sales and account managers, misaligned incentives can cause overselling at the outset. Field sales may prioritize short-term targets without considering the long-term impact, leading to poor handovers and missed upsell opportunities. To mitigate this, an option is to tie part of the incentives to post-sale outcomes, such as customer usage, retention, or upselling.

Hybrid models that combine recurring revenue with upfront fees pose another challenge. Sales teams may over-discount one component to secure a deal, undermining long-term revenue. Balance incentives to prioritize recurring revenue, which often holds greater long-term value.

Finally, continuously monitor and refine the incentive structure to prevent unintended consequences. For example, a focus on large deals might reduce attention to smaller but highly profitable opportunities. Regular reviews ensure that incentives remain aligned with both pricing strategy and business goals, promoting sustainable growth and profitability.

SUMMARY

- **Prepare the pricing page (with or without prices displayed):** Whether or not to display pricing on your website depends on your sales model, customer expectations, and ability to estimate pricing online. While transparency can build trust and boost conversions, it may reduce interaction and reveal pricing to competitors; regardless, present your offering and value clearly, and continuously test and improve the pricing page for maximum engagement.

- **Compile a sales playbook, in particular, value-selling arguments and counterarguments:** To enable effective value-based selling, equip your sales team with a well-maintained sales playbook containing value messaging, objection handling, and pricing guidelines. The material should not focus on features but on customer benefits, proof points, and tailored arguments that reflect what truly drives customer decisions.

- **Leverage behavioral pricing concepts on the pricing page and in the sales material:** Psychological pricing tactics, such as anchor pricing, default options, and the "magic of the middle," help influence customer perceptions and decision-making. These concepts should be carefully integrated into both the pricing page and sales materials to maximize conversions while maintaining customer trust.

- **Prepare a delegation of authority and an escalation path:** Clear guidelines should define the extent of packaging, discounting, and contract flexibility that sales teams can offer, reducing unnecessary approvals while maintaining pricing discipline. An escalation path ensures deals receive the necessary oversight, balancing sales agility with control.

- **Align incentives with company objectives:** Align incentive models with your pricing strategy to drive the right sales behaviors, balancing growth and profitability while addressing potential challenges like excessive discounting and poor handovers between sales roles. Continuously review and refine the model to spot and mitigate unintended outcomes.

CHAPTER 8

Price Governance

ENSURE TRANSPARENCY

Complete visibility and control over your pricing are essential. After all, you can't change what you can't see. To manage pricing effectively across your business, it's essential to define the right metrics, at the right level of detail, for the right audience, and to monitor them at an appropriate cadence. This requires implementing dashboards and reporting systems to provide every relevant team member access to the insights they need to make consistent, well-informed decisions.

Creating transparency starts with capturing data at the necessary level of granularity to enable meaningful analysis and conclusions. To do this, your product and customer data must accurately reflect how you sell. Your stock-keeping unit (SKU) hierarchy should match the granularity of your packaging and pricing to ensure your product and price data are aligned. Simply put, each product must be priced at the most detailed level at which it is sold. Take, for instance, a business that sells packs of three water bottles for 8 USD, but also offers individual bottles at 3 USD each. If both options are available to customers, there should be separate SKUs for the single bottle and the three-pack of bottles. We've seen even large, established companies struggle to track what they've sold to customers due to misalignment between product and pricing data.

The same logic applies to customer data. Be sure to collect the customer characteristics that influence pricing. These attributes can help explain price variations and serve as the foundation for more advanced price differentiation down the line.

AUTOMATION AND TOOLS

Your pricing strategy should support—not hinder—your sales team. Aim to systematize and automate as much of your packaging, pricing, and approval workflows as possible, including governance areas like discount tracking and special terms & conditions. While using offline tools such as Excel for pricing guidance and relying on email-based approvals may work in the early startup phase, these manual processes should be replaced with automation as soon as your business begins to scale.

One way of making the quotation process better is to introduce a configure, price, quote (CPQ) tool. These tools become important if there are multiple salespersons and/or complex offerings. A CPQ ensures that each step in the sales process is carried out according to a standard playbook and that pricing and configurations are accurate. Listed below are some helpful functionalities to consider:[57]

- Product configuration. The ability to easily configure complex products, services, or bundles with multiple options, ensuring the right combination is selected for customers.
- Pricing management. Flexible pricing rules that accommodate various price and discount models, and ensure accurate, dynamic pricing based on business needs.
- Quote generation. Fast, automated creation of accurate and professional quotes and proposals, reflecting correct product configurations, pricing, and terms.
- Approval workflow. Automated workflows for pricing approvals, discounts, and escalations, ensuring compliance with pricing policies and preventing errors.
- Integration with CRM and ERP systems. Seamless integration with existing CRM (e.g., Salesforce) and ERP systems to ensure data consistency, streamline processes, and avoid duplication.

More niche features to consider are:

- Deal benchmarking. See directly within the tool how the quote compares with similar quotes.
- Incentive calculations. Make sales incentives visible as part of the quoting process to show the salespersons how the quotes impact their incentives.

MEASURE AND TUNE

To continuously develop the packaging and pricing, select and monitor KPIs that provide insights into the pricing performance. You'll find the most common set of KPIs listed below. Note that most of these KPIs are for general business performance and not only for pricing, but the impact of pricing on these KPIs is important to understand and monitor to inform pricing decisions. The main KPIs are:

- **Annual Recurring Revenue (ARR):** Tracks predictable, recurring revenue from subscriptions. Effective packaging and pricing directly impact ARR by either increasing the value of subscriptions or reducing churn.
- **Average Revenue Per Account (ARPA):** Shows the average annual revenue generated per customer. Increasing ARPA can be achieved through higher-tier pricing, upselling, or adding premium features that customers are willing to pay for.
- **Churn Rate:** Measures the percentage of customers who cancel their subscriptions. High churn can indicate that pricing is too high or customers don't perceive enough value, signaling a need for price and packaging adjustments.
- **Net Revenue Retention (NRR):** Tracks how much revenue is retained from existing customers after accounting for upgrades, downgrades, and churn. High NRR suggests that pricing is effective in encouraging customer retention and expansion through upsells.
- **Win/Conversion Rate and Reasons:** This metric tracks the percentage of leads that convert into paying customers. Clear, attractive pricing can boost conversion rates and shorten the sales cycle.
- **Customer Acquisition Cost (CAC):** This metric measures the cost of acquiring a new customer and indicates whether your pricing aligns with your target market. A high CAC relative to willingness to pay suggests inefficiencies, while a drop in CAC after adjustments signals improved alignment with customer expectations.
- **Customer Lifetime Value (CLTV):** The total revenue a customer will generate during their relationship with your business. Pricing strategies should aim to increase CLTV by encouraging longer customer retention and higher spending through upsells or premium plans.

Other valuable data to track to improve pricing performance are:

- **Discounting levels (including non-price discounts, such as deviations from standard terms and conditions):** Which customers received more discounts or deviating terms and conditions, and why? If there was a condition for the discount, is that condition still valid?

- **Win/loss reasons:** As a complement to the win/conversion rate: Where do you win/lose? Against who? And why?
- **Churn reasons:** As a complement to the churn rate: Which customers churn? Do they churn to a competitor? Which one? And why?
- **NPS/customer satisfaction:** How satisfied are the customers? Who are the most and least satisfied customers? Why?

All KPIs should ideally be possible to analyze in different cuts, such as industry or tenure. Based on experience, few companies follow up on all of the above, which limits the available information on pricing performance and thereby makes it difficult to perform systematic analyses. Therefore, start sampling and monitoring the data as early as possible, and use it to refine your packaging and pricing.

HEAD OF PRICING

A key reason pricing often falls through the cracks is the absence of clear ownership or prioritization. Without clear ownership, pricing becomes an afterthought or a reactive process, often executed without the support of data-driven insights.

To address this, a "head of pricing" should coordinate all activities related to setting and achieving optimal pricing. Their responsibilities encompass defining and tracking pricing KPIs while ensuring these are monitored consistently. This includes gathering pricing intelligence from customers and competitors, as well as leading the development of the packaging and pricing. They are also tasked with monitoring key metrics, such as win/loss rates, churn, and discounting trends, providing necessary training to align teams with pricing strategies, and ensuring the timely execution of price adjustments, such as price increases.

Supporting these activities requires collecting accurate and relevant data to inform pricing decisions. Ensuring data quality and incorporating appropriate segmentation is crucial for meaningful analysis. By managing these elements effectively, the head of pricing ensures that pricing decisions are both strategic and data-driven.

The head of pricing can report to various functions, including the CEO, sales, marketing, product, or finance, depending on the organization's structure and strategic priorities. There is no widely accepted best practice in which role the head of pricing should report; each reporting structure has its unique advantages and challenges, as illustrated in Figure 8.1. Establishing clear ownership and accountability enables pricing to evolve from a reactive task into a strategic lever for driving growth and profitability.

Reporting To	Pros	Cons
CEO	Direct alignment with overall business strategy, faster decision-making	May lack focus on detailed pricing tactics; CEO might have limited pricing expertise
Sales	Strong focus on revenue growth and sales alignment, ensures pricing drives revenue	Risk of pricing becoming too sales-driven, neglecting product or market factors
Marketing	Alignment with market positioning and customer segmentation strategies	Potential disconnect between pricing and revenue goals; less focus on financials
Product	Direct connection with product strategy, ensuring pricing reflects product value	Risk of overlooking revenue or customer acquisition goals in favor of product features
Finance	Strong focus on profitability and cost structures, ensuring pricing is financially sound	Risk of being overly focused on margins, potentially ignoring market competitiveness or customer value

Figure 8.1: Pros and cons of different reporting lines for a head of pricing.

FINE-TUNING AND EXPERIMENTS

Schumpeter, often referred to as the father of innovation, identified five types of innovation: the development of new products, the introduction of new production methods, the cultivation of new markets, the acquisition of new resources, and organizational reforms.[58] However, there has been a suggestion that pricing should be considered another source of innovation.[59] Viewing pricing as an innovation highlights the need for regular updates, much like any other product, process, or organizational practice.

Pricing innovation is an ongoing process involving experimentation with new packaging and pricing models. As your offering evolves and customers' willingness to pay shifts, it becomes critical to routinely fine-tune packaging and pricing. This requires research to test and validate concepts, ensuring alignment with market dynamics and customer needs. Such updates should be data-driven, leveraging both primary and secondary data sources, such as internal transaction data and direct customer or prospect feedback.

For smaller changes or when dealing with a high volume of customers or visitors, simple testing methods like A/B testing can be effective. For example, you can present different pricing models or price points to separate groups and evaluate performance based on preset criteria. Key to any experiment is ensuring a sufficient sample size for meaningful conclusions, defining success criteria in advance, and having a plan for the next steps if results don't meet expectations.

For larger changes to your offering or price model, or when qualitative insights are needed, customer interviews and surveys become indispensable. These methods allow you to gather nuanced feedback directly from customers, which can guide your pricing innovation efforts. In these interviews, you could gather the following information:

- **Customer information:** Sample information about the segment (including size, industry, etc.), solution, add-ons, and usage.
- **Needs and buying process:** Assess the buying process and buying criteria.
- **Satisfaction with the current solution:** Understand customer satisfaction, how the company/other provider meets their needs, and if something appears to be missing.
- **Feature value:** Investigate the perceived value of individual functionalities and service elements.
- **Offering concept:** Evaluate the perceived value, pros, and cons of concrete packaging options, and understand preferences.
- **Price questions:** Get input on price model options and willingness to pay/price levels.
- **Closing questions:** Overall satisfaction/NPS and final remarks.

The price questions are toward the end. This is to avoid biases in the other answers because asking questions about prices may impact the questions that follow. If an interviewee thinks the responses are used for pricing, there is a risk they could lie about their usage, needs, and willingness to pay. In the interviews, it is helpful to bring concrete concepts that interviewees can comment on and react to. Prepare mockups of the packages and descriptions of the price model that you will show the interviewee.

It's also wise to simulate any radically new approaches and test them with one or more subsets of customers before allowing any rollout across your entire customer base. Netflix, for example, leverages experimentation on changes to their customer experience to market-test them before rolling them out across the base.[60]

A piece of advice is also to reach out to companies that have completed the changes you are planning but in other verticals to get some input. For example, if you're planning to introduce usage-based pricing for your manufacturing robot, reach out to a company that has introduced usage-based pricing for robotic lawnmowers. People are normally open to sharing their experience or insights with noncompetitors.

INTERNAL PRICING STAKEHOLDERS
AND CHANGE MANAGEMENT

When running a pricing project, you should involve a cross-functional team to ensure the new packaging and pricing can be implemented by gathering input from pricing stakeholders. The team should at least cover product, sales, and marketing, but ideally also finance and other functions/persons with relevant insights into pricing. A key success factor for implementation is that all those functions believe in the new packaging and pricing. To avoid making the project too slow, limit the key decision-makers to about three to five, while a broader set of people can be involved where and when needed.

Keep in mind the change management aspect when introducing new pricing. For example, transitioning from a one-time product price or perpetual license to a subscription model represents a significant shift, as does moving to a differentiated multi-package offering or adopting usage-based pricing instead of user-based pricing. If you make larger changes, ensure that you plan for the required change management.

Change management involves several key components to ensure a successful transition.[61] It begins with planning, where the scope, objectives, and implementation roadmap are defined. Stakeholder engagement is critical, as it involves understanding and addressing the concerns of those affected by the change. Clear communication throughout the process is necessary to explain the change, its benefits, and its impact. Training and support help employees adapt by providing the necessary resources and knowledge. During implementation, the change is executed with continuous monitoring and adjustments as needed. Feedback and monitoring ensure the change is received effectively, while reinforcement through recognition and ongoing support helps sustain the change long term.

CUSTOMER MIGRATION

In connection with any larger packaging and price revision, there is normally a need to migrate customers to the new monetization model. There are some key considerations to think about in those situations. First, map each customer to the new offering and price model and calculate what the change will be in terms of price level. Then classify each customer based on their price sensitivity. Based on these exercises, you can determine the migration strategy per customer. The main migration strategies are listed below.

- **New accounts only:** New pricing applies only to new customers, leaving existing ones on legacy plans. This low-risk approach is ideal for fast-growing companies and allows for real-world testing without upsetting current users. However, it slows revenue impact and creates internal complexity by maintaining multiple pricing models.

- **Immediate full price increase:** All customers are moved to the new pricing at once. It's simple, fast, and provides immediate revenue gains. It's best suited for modest increases or when customers show a high willingness to pay. The downside is the risk of churn or dissatisfaction, so strong value communication is essential.
- **Phase price increases across multiple years:** Customers transition gradually to the new price. This approach eases acceptance of significant increases and minimizes churn risk, but it delays full financial impact and adds complexity to managing multiple price points.
- **Time out price changes with major product updates:** Price increases are aligned with feature launches, making the value exchange clear. Ideal for larger increases, this method depends on the timely delivery of product improvements and may delay pricing changes if roadmaps slip.
- **"Grandfather" strategic accounts:** Key or dormant customers keep existing pricing, often to avoid negotiation or churn. This preserves relationships but delays monetization and may create inconsistency if not carefully managed.

Next, prepare a clear value proposition to communicate the rationale behind the migration, emphasizing the benefits for customers. Highlight any new features or improvements associated with the migration to make the changes more appealing. However, it's essential to plan for potential negative reactions and prepare concessions, such as temporary discounts, free add-ons, or temporary upgrades to a higher-tier package. Downgrades to lower packages should be a last resort. Additionally, consider implementing an escalation plan for concessions and, if necessary, provide special incentives to key individuals involved in the migration process.

Determine the timing for the migration and establish KPIs to measure success. Common KPIs include the number of customers up for renewal, the number of customers accepting the new pricing, targeted versus actual ARR after price adjustments, and churn or contraction rates.

Finally, create a follow-up strategy detailing who will monitor progress, the frequency of reviews, and actions to be taken if progress falls short of expectations. A structured approach ensures accountability and timely adjustments to keep the migration on track.

PRICE INCREASE PROCESS

A key process to consider is the price increase process, which is essential for successfully implementing price adjustments. This process shares many similarities with the migration process discussed in the previous section and typically unfolds in three main steps:

- **Determine targets:** Set price increase targets at the customer or product level, considering factors like price elasticity and customer-specific or product-specific strategies. Conduct thorough analyses of your customer base to understand current price levels and price sensitivity, and use these insights to establish realistic uplift targets.
- **Prepare for implementation:** Define the level of discretion allowed for discounting price increases and set clear escalation rules. Decide which customers require negotiation (if any) versus those where prices can be increased directly. Prepare communication materials, conduct necessary training, and inform the customer-facing teams, such as support, to ensure consistent messaging. If needed, consider introducing special incentives to support the success of the price-increase initiative.
- **Develop an execution plan:** Create a detailed plan outlining when and how to approach each customer. Prepare tailored arguments for potential negotiations and establish a monitoring system to track customer feedback, interactions, and negotiation outcomes. Schedule regular progress reviews to adjust targets, provide support to the team, and ensure the process stays on track.

Similarly as for the migration, define and monitor KPIs, such as the number of customers subject to price increases, the number of customers accepting the price increase, targeted versus actual ARR after price increases, and churn or contraction rates. As with many other activities, price increases are easier to manage when conducted regularly, as frequent adjustments help normalize the process for both your team and your customers.

PRICE UPDATE COMMUNICATION

When migrating existing customers or increasing prices, clear and empathetic communication is essential. Be transparent about when the changes will take effect and why they are necessary, focusing on reasons such as added investments in features, content, or product improvements. However, be thoughtful about what you refer to so you don't create an expectation of price reductions when the underlying cost goes down. For example, if you state a raw material price increase as a reason, the same day that very same raw material decreases in price, your customers would want you to reduce your price.

Additionally, highlight the value customers will gain from the increase, such as new benefits or enhancements driven by the additional revenue. If the changes include a packaging and pricing redesign, communicate any updates, such as unlimited users or restructured tiers, and explain how existing plans map to the new structure. Make it easy for customers to understand what they're moving to and what the changes mean for them.

Tailor the message by segment. High-value or strategic accounts may require one-on-one outreach, while others can be addressed with automated emails and FAQs. Segment-specific messaging ensures relevance, minimizes confusion, and shows you've considered the impact on different groups.

Prepare internal teams, especially support, sales, and customer success, with clear explanations, objection-handling guides, and potential concessions (e.g., temporary discounts, free add-ons, temporary upgrades, etc.). Ensuring your teams are aligned and confident is just as important as the external message.

Avoid using vague, overly apologetic, or defensive language. Be confident, clear, concise, and respectful. Acknowledge that price changes can be frustrating, but frame the conversation around added value and your long-term commitment to improving the customer experience.

Give customers ample notice and consider offering options to ease the transition, such as locking in current prices by upgrading to a premium package or renewing early. Maintain a positive tone to build trust, show appreciation for their loyalty, and ensure there's a clear way for customers to ask questions or share concerns.

Ensure everything around the communication is well-prepared, as this is a critical opportunity to reinforce trust. You only get one chance. Make it count.

A CULTURE OF VALUE-BASED PRICING

Establishing a culture centered on value-based pricing is ultimately the responsibility of the CEO. It begins with the CEO instilling this mindset within the leadership team and ensuring that actions consistently reflect the company's pricing philosophy. The core principles of a value-based pricing culture include:

- Treating monetization as a key organizational capability—one that is continuously developed and optimized over time.

- Incorporating discussions around product value and pricing early in the product development cycle to ensure the packaging and pricing are aligned with customer needs and customer's willingness to pay.
- Empowering leaders to walk away from bad deals and supporting the sales team in doing so is reinforced through incentives and delegation of authority structures.

Fostering such a culture is not easy. It demands commitment, discipline, and consistency, as a culture of value-based pricing is fragile and can quickly erode if not actively supported. However, the benefits are substantial. A global study by the consultancy Simon-Kucher[62] found that companies where the CEO is actively involved in pricing tend to be more profitable and have greater pricing power than those without an involved CEO.

UPDATE CADENCE

Pricing should be refined continuously. Daily refinements are mostly related to decisions on where in the offering structure new features or updates should be, fine-tune the price levels, or review how to best present the offering and prices to a customer. However, you should make a more thorough review at least every six months, where you review the commercial performance by digging into achieved prices, win/loss data, and churn information, while also summarizing feedback from customers and the sales team. This information is then used to make larger adjustments if needed, but it does not necessarily require a full packaging and pricing overhaul.

Additionally, there will be times when an overhaul of the monetization model is required. We suggest aiming at making an overhaul at least every two to three years to consider the change in product performance, customer needs, and competitive landscape during that time. Nevertheless, there may be events that require an immediate overhaul of the packaging and pricing. This could include new competitors entering the market, new types of products being available, significant changes in competitors' pricing, new technology available, economic shocks, or events changing customer preferences. It is therefore advantageous if the organization knows how to run a packaging and pricing redesign to ensure it can be carried out when needed.

SUMMARY

- **Collect commercial data systematically:** Systematic collection of commercial data, including pricing performance, discount trends, win/loss analysis, and customer behavior, is essential for making informed pricing decisions.
- **Appoint a head of pricing:** A dedicated "head of pricing" ensures that pricing remains a priority, coordinating pricing intelligence, KPIs, and adjustments across functions. This role drives data-driven pricing decisions and continuous improvements in the packaging and pricing.
- **Prepare an approach for pricing experiments and research:** A structured approach to pricing experiments, such as A/B testing and customer interviews/surveys, enables continuous refinement of the packaging and pricing. Testing new pricing strategies ensures alignment with customer needs and a willingness to pay while minimizing risk.
- **Plan the customer migration (if needed):** When introducing new packaging and pricing, a successful customer migration requires careful mapping of price impact and sensitivity, clear value communication, a tailored migration strategy, and a structured follow-up with defined KPIs to manage risk and ensure adoption.
- **Introduce a price-increase process:** A successful price-increase process involves setting clear uplift targets, preparing communication and escalation guidelines, executing with tailored customer plans, and tracking KPIs to ensure adoption. This should be done regularly to normalize the activity.
- **Build a culture of value-based pricing:** A value-based pricing culture, cultivated by the CEO, treats monetization as a core capability, embeds pricing early in product development, and empowers teams to walk away from bad deals—driving long-term profitability and pricing power.

CHAPTER 9

Special Topics

MANAGED SERVICES AND SERVICE CONTRACTS

If your offering includes the work of individuals, such as consultants or technicians, there are specific considerations to keep in mind. In the context of subscriptions, these offerings often fall under service contracts or managed services, which differ significantly in terms of scope and responsibility.

Service contracts are reactive and task-oriented, with the provider delivering services on demand while the customer retains overall responsibility. Managed services, on the other hand, are proactive and ongoing, with the provider taking full responsibility for monitoring, managing, and optimizing systems to ensure performance and continuous improvement.

When developing the packaging and pricing for these services, it is essential to clearly define the scope to ensure customers understand what is included and expected. This may involve service components, such as response times, resolution times, uptime guarantees, and personalized options like dedicated advisors or customized tests and simulations. Specify what is included and excluded to prevent scope creep, and outline additional charges for services outside the agreement.

To maintain profitability, evaluate both fixed costs (e.g., tools and licenses) and variable costs (e.g., labor and resource usage). Regularly monitor service utilization to ensure pricing reflects actual effort. Customers with intensive support needs may justify higher fees, while usage caps or thresholds can control overuse. Additionally, pricing should factor in risk and liability, with services offering SLAs or guarantees incorporating margins to mitigate these risks.

HARDWARE AS A SERVICE (HAAS)

If your offering includes a hardware component, the overall pricing approach remains similar to software offerings. However, it's crucial to consider features tied specifically to hardware and software. For hardware, differentiation could come from offering various products or performance levels.

The main difference lies in handling hardware costs. Since hardware has significant physical costs, start by analyzing costs and margins to set pricing guardrails. Key considerations include the bill of materials (BOM) payback period and the share of hardware as a percentage of the total price.

The BOM payback period (BPP) is a critical metric for HaaS businesses.[63] It measures the number of months before recurring customer payments offset the upfront hardware costs.[64] Companies typically aim for a BPP of twelve to eighteen months. For instance, if hardware costs 9,000 USD to build and customers pay 600 USD per month, the BPP is fifteen months, the point where hardware costs are roughly covered. This metric ties directly to unit economics, making a strong understanding of these economics essential for scalability.

So what's a good BPP? It depends on the product and desired margins, but a range of six to twenty-four months is generally reasonable.

- **Very Good:** Six to twelve months. A best-in-class BPP for a solution with low-cost hardware, a strong software layer, and a complementary service package.
- **Good:** Twelve to eighteen months. Many HaaS models with this BPP are performing well.
- **Decent:** Eighteen to twenty-four months. Companies can make it work, but margins may suffer.
- **Challenging:** Over twenty-four months. Financing becomes difficult, and making the interest calculations work becomes challenging.

Exceptions to these benchmarks are long-term contracts (over three years) and government contracts, where extended BPPs can still be profitable.

Besides BPP, another rule of thumb to consider when setting the price is how the share of the total price allocated between hardware and software varies depending on the total price level.[65] In general, for more expensive pieces of equipment, hardware is a bigger part of the full package price. A HaaS package might cost 100 USD in total, such as for a sensor, where hardware makes up 10 percent and software 90 percent of the total. On the other hand, in a HaaS package that might cost one million USD in total, such as for a 3D printer, hardware makes up 80 percent and software 20 percent of the total. This is, of course, a simplification. Charges such as shipping, maintenance, and accessories are also included but provide an indication of the proportions between hardware and software fees.

TWO-SIDED MARKETS

A two-sided market is a platform that connects two distinct user groups, such as buyers and sellers, where the value for one group increases as the other group grows. Examples include Uber (drivers and riders) and Airbnb (hosts and guests). Packaging and pricing typically differ for each side, requiring a balance of their needs and dynamics, which may involve separate packages and price models.

Network effects are crucial since the platform's value grows as more users join each side, driving further participation. To stimulate this growth, the more price-sensitive side is often subsidized to boost engagement, enhancing the platform's appeal to the other side. This cross-side subsidization involves charging the side with a higher willingness to pay (e.g., advertisers or sellers) while offering lower or free access to the other side (e.g., buyers). Tailored packaging and pricing maximize engagement and fairness.

Early-stage platforms prioritize achieving critical mass, addressing the "chicken-and-egg" problem by incentivizing one side (e.g., discounts for buyers) until both sides are active. Price elasticity and willingness to pay guide adjustments to sustain participation. As platforms mature, the focus shifts typically from growth to monetization. Early subsidies are phased out in favor of optimized revenue streams across both sides, with competitor pricing informing strategies to maintain differentiation. However, overcharging one side can erode trust or attract regulatory scrutiny, jeopardizing long-term sustainability.

BUSINESS TO CONSUMER (B2C)

B2C pricing is typically simpler and more transparent, often relying on fixed subscription rates. Purchasing decisions are made quickly and are driven by individual consumer needs rather than complex organizational requirements. B2C pricing strategies frequently employ freemium models or promotional offers to attract users. Customer support is often self-service-oriented, utilizing online resources, FAQs, and chatbots.

Additionally, B2C pricing and sales are often subject to stricter regulations. For instance, price increase clauses may face tighter control, and requirements for clear and timely price communication can also be more stringent.

ONBOARDING FEES

Some services, in particular within B2B, require onboarding in terms of system configuration, training, etc. These are often charged as an upfront fee, commonly referred to as an "onboarding fee" or "deployment fee," typically based on time and materials, as the subscription offering remains the primary product customers seek. In some cases, onboarding can be extensive, involving numerous users, complex integrations, and multiple customizations, which can result in significant costs.

Based on experience, these are the reactions on different levels (the percentage is the onboarding fee in relation to the annual contract value [ACV]):

- **0–25 percent of ACV:** Accepted with almost no questions.
- **25–50 percent of ACV:** Accepted, but potentially with a few questions.
- **50–100 percent of ACV:** Accepted, but normally with multiple questions. Be prepared to explain and sell the onboarding.
- **>100 percent of ACV:** This tends to become a separate sales process. Expect your customers to want to understand and negotiate all deliverables. For onboarding priced as multiples of the ACV, be prepared that the onboarding cost might be negotiated more than the actual subscription price.

A helpful strategy to facilitate the sales process for an expensive onboarding is to offer one or more productized onboarding options, ideally with at least one priced below 50 percent of the ACV. This allows you to position the higher onboarding cost in the sales dialogue as a result of additional customization, special integrations, or other factors specific to the buyer's needs. By framing the onboarding cost around the customers' unique requirements, they can better understand the added value and price associated with those customizations, making the pricing easier to justify.

SUMMARY

- **Set service scope and determine cost to serve (if managed services or service contracts):** When pricing managed services, clearly define scope, responsibilities, and service levels, and ensure pricing reflects both fixed and variable costs, customer usage, and associated risk. Unlike reactive service contracts, managed services require proactive delivery and full accountability.

- **Set BPP (if HaaS offering):** BPP is an important metric that determines how long it takes for recurring payments to offset upfront hardware costs. A target BPP of twelve to eighteen months is generally ideal to maintain strong unit economics and sustainable growth.

- **Review hardware/software split of total price (if HaaS offering):** The proportion of total pricing allocated to hardware versus software in a HaaS model depends on the overall cost; software is typically a larger share of the total for products with a lower total price.

- **Consider potential cross-side subsidization (if two-sided markets):** In two-sided platforms, pricing must balance the needs of both user groups. Oftentimes, the more price-sensitive side is subsidized to fuel network effects early on, and then it gradually shifts toward monetization as the platform matures.

- **Review B2C-specific considerations (if consumers are targeted):** B2C pricing tends to be simpler and more transparent, often using freemium or promotional models, with faster buying decisions and self-service support. There are usually tighter regulatory requirements, especially around price increases and communication.

- **Understand and address onboarding fee size versus ACV (if onboarding is required):** Onboarding services—often charged as a one-time fee—vary in acceptance based on size relative to ACV. Fees under 25 percent are typically unchallenged, while higher costs require justification or detailed negotiation; offering productized onboarding options helps streamline sales and clarify value.

Summary

Finally, there won't be a single "correct way" to package and price your product. Several viable approaches can lead to a successful business, each with its own set of advantages and drawbacks. You'll likely need to refine your packaging and pricing over time, based on feedback from customers and internal stakeholders. Expect to face multiple trade-offs and occasional tough choices. It's a journey that relies as much on creativity as it does on data and analysis. What's certain is that investing in this capability can unlock significant value for both your company and your customers.

Depending on where you are on your pricing journey, you may want to address all aspects in this book or just a selection. Below is the summary checklist from all of the chapters. Best of luck!

CHAPTER SUMMARIES

1. **Business objectives:**
   - Set overall goals for the commercial operations
   - Determine key trade-offs (e.g., growth vs. profitability)
   - Get everyone aligned on the strategy
2. **Customer segmentation:**
   - Segment customers based on their needs
   - Understand customers' buying processes, involved stakeholders, and buying criteria
   - Determine your positioning

3. **Channel strategy:**
   - Select preferred sales channel(s) per segment and market
   - Identify and mitigate potential channel conflicts
   - Select partners and design a partner program (if you use indirect sales)
   - Consider freemium or free trial (if you use self-service)
   - Account for key considerations for each channel
4. **Offering model:**
   - Longlist available features and their corresponding benefits
   - Determine the packaging approach based on customer needs and channel strategy
   - Design packages based on feature value and adoption
   - Define the upsell path for customers
   - Consider all components in the offering (e.g., support, services, hardware, third-party products)
5. **Price model:**
   - Select price metric(s)
   - Determine modality, granularity, and structure
   - Evaluate price models based on value to customers and your business
   - Consider a fair usage clause (if needed)
   - Set price models for add-ons and secondary products (if needed)
   - Determine contract duration and billing frequency
   - Review the terms and conditions
6. **Price level:**
   - Use the most suitable price-setting methods (ideally multiple methods)
   - Consider price differentiation (both on a list price and discount level)
   - Develop discount guidelines (considering both amount and type)
7. **Price communication:**
   - Prepare the pricing page (with or without prices displayed)
   - Compile a sales playbook, in particular, value selling arguments and counterarguments
   - Leverage behavioral pricing concepts on the pricing page and in the sales material
   - Prepare a delegation of authority and an escalation path
   - Align incentives with company objectives
8. **Price governance:**
   - Collect commercial data systematically
   - Appoint a head of pricing
   - Prepare an approach for pricing experiments and research

- Plan the customer migration (if needed)
- Introduce a price increase process
- Build a culture of value-based pricing

9. **Special topics:**
   - Set service scope and determine cost to serve (if managed services or service contracts)
   - Set BPP (if HaaS offering)
   - Review hardware/software split of total price (if HaaS offering)
   - Consider potential cross-side subsidization (if two-sided markets)
   - Review B2C-specific considerations (if consumers are targeted)
   - Understand and address the onboarding fee size versus ACV (if onboarding is required)

Overview of Acronyms Used

ACV = Annual contract value
AI = Artificial intelligence
AP = Accounts payable
API = Application programming interface
ARPA = Average revenue per account
ARR = Annual recurring revenue
B2B = Business-to-business
B2C = Business-to-consumer
BOM = Bill of materials
BPP = Bill of materials payback period
CAC = Customer acquisition cost
CLG = Community-led growth
CPI = Consumer Price Index
CPQ = Configure, price, quote
CRM = Customer relationship management
CLTV = Customer lifetime value
EBITDA = Earnings before interest, taxes, depreciation, and amortization
ERP = Enterprise resource planning
GRR = Gross retention rate
HaaS = Hardware as a Service
ICP = Ideal customer profile

IPA = Importance-performance analysis
KPI = Key performance indicator
KYC = Know your customer
NPS = Net promoter score
NRR = Net retention rate
PLG = Product-led growth
PO = Purchase order
RFP = Request for proposal
ROI = Return on investment
SaaS = Software as a Service
SKU = Stock-keeping unit
SLA = Service-level agreement
WTP = Willingness to pay
XaaS = Anything as a Service

Acknowledgments

A book is not written by itself. There are several people involved, one way or another.

For content, I would like to thank foremost all the companies I have had the honor to work with throughout the years. Furthermore, I want to thank all the mentors I have had throughout my pricing career, including current and previous colleagues at Simon-Kucher and Axholmen. Last, I'd like to thank the pricing community that shares new insights and thoughts on pricing questions.

For feedback on the text, I would like to thank in particular (in order of when they provided feedback, from first to last): Slava Ceornea, Felix Magnusson, Peter Dahl, Filip Schager, Mia Johnston, Emma Dahlin, Ola Qviberg, Frank Majgren, Johannes Brunegård, Richard Glimstedt, Willem Dewulf, Peter O. Bäck, Dylan Vest, Christian Lardon, Ana Calvo, Carla Mörée Calvo, Petter Mörée, Steffen Ketterer, John Elf, Johan Tordsson, Karl Holm, Magnus Serratusell Wallin, Saper Şahbaz, Elin Norell, and Wilma Eriksson.

Last, but far from least, I want to thank my friends and family for their support during the whole process. Thank you!

About the Author

FELIX MÖRÉE is an expert in pricing, having worked in the field for almost a decade. Throughout this time, he has worked foremost with marketing, packaging, pricing, and sales of subscriptions. Felix has a background as a consultant at Simon-Kucher and Axholmen. Before that, he pursued a double degree in engineering physics and economics at Lund University. Prior to this book, he published four books on pricing and profitability in Sweden and Finland, of which the book *Ta Betalt!* won the marketing book of the year 2019 in Sweden.

For any feedback on the content of this book, please email felix@ PricingPotential.com or visit the website PricingPotential.com.

Notes

1   "The Five Biggest Pricing Mistakes Saas Companies Make," *SaaS Mag*, August 17, 2023, https://www.
    saasmag.com/five-biggest-saas-pricing-mistakes/.

2   Based on packaging and pricing redesigns for subscription businesses, impact may vary depending on
    factors such as pricing maturity, competitive landscape, implementation, etc.

3   Marc Brysbaert, "How Many Words Do We Read per Minute? A Review and Meta-Analysis of Reading
    Rate," *Journal of Memory and Language* 109 (2019).

4   Sarah L. C. Clapp, "The Beginnings of Subscription Publication in the Seventeenth Century," *Modern
    Philology* 29, no. 2 (1931).

5   Nick Brown, "The History of SaaS | The New Digital Revolution, Explained," Accelerate, published
    December 6, 2021, https://accelerate.agency/the-history-of-saas.

6   Tien Tzu, *Subscribed* (Portfolio Penguin, 2018).

7   The demand curve has the following formula: Volume = 5,000 – 10 × Price.

8   Profit = (Price – Cost) × Volume, meaning (300 – 100) × 2,000 = 400,000.

9   Profit = (Price – Cost) × Volume for each of the 3 price levels, meaning (200 – 100) × 1,000 + (300 – 100)
    × 1,000 + (400 – 100) × 1,000 = 600,000.

10 The profit is calculated as the area of the triangle, meaning (500 – 100) × 4,000 ÷ 2 = 800,000.

11 Madhavan Ramanujam and Georg Tacke, *Monetizing Innovation* (Wiley, 2016).

12 Product/market fit means being in a good market with a product that can satisfy that market. See: Marc
    Andreessen, "The Only Thing That Matters," Pmarchive, posted June 25, 2007, https://pmarchive.com/
    guide_to_startups_part4.html.

13 Dan Olsen, *The Lean Product Playbook: How to Innovate with Minimum Viable Products and Rapid
    Customer Feedback* (Wiley, 2015).

14   Read more about different AP automation solutions at, for example, Gartner: https://www.gartner.com/reviews/market/accounts-payable-invoice-automation-solutions.

15   Alice Darla, "Spotify's Bold Profit Move: How Price Hikes and Subscriber Growth Drive Its Path to Profitability," Neon Music, published November 13, 2024, https://neonmusic.co.uk/spotifys-bold-profit-move-how-price-hikes-and-subscriber-growth-drive-its-path-to-profitability.

16   Brad Feld, "Rule of 40 for a Healthy SaaS Company," Feld Thoughts, April 9, 2015, https://feld.com/archives/2015/02/rule-40-healthy-saas-company; Fred Wilson, "The Rule of 40% for a Healthy SaaS Business," AVC, April 2015.

17   The assessment is based on desk research of their commercial strategy in April 2025. Their actual strategy may differ.

18   The assessment is based on desk research of their commercial strategy in April 2025. Their actual strategy may differ.

19   Multiple examples of this comparison circulate online without any source on the original creator. Please reach out in case you know the original creator.

20   Robert Bradford and M. Dana Baldwin, "How Many Market Segments Should You Have to Be Successful?," CSSP, retrieved March 2025, https://www.cssp.com/how-many-market-segments-should-you-have-to-be-successful/?srsltid=AfmBOor8zOeyXYVqIOHpaLUGYjPNpNIEXfVq3nXUTHTaPvu_GkTpnenn.

21   Tim Bock, "How to Work Out the Number of Segments for a Market Segmentation," QResearchSoftware, retrieved March 2025, https://www.qresearchsoftware.com/how-to-work-out-the-number-of-segments-for-a-market-segmentation.

22   A clear and accepted segmentation strategy will reduce the risk of derailing the roadmap due to not spending time on developing features for customers that are not ICP.

23   Anthony W. Ulwick, Jobs to Be Done: Theory to Practice (Idea Bite Press, 2016).

24   John A. Martilla and John C. James, "Importance-Performance Analysis," The Journal of Marketing 41, no. 1, (1977): 77–79, https://slunik.slu.se/kursfiler/F%C3%960349/10294.1314/Martilla_James_1977.pdf.

25   "A Positioning Deep-Dive with April Dunford," Oxx, published July 17, 2023, https://www.oxx.vc/news/video-a-positioning-deep-dive-with-april-dunford/.

26   Based on desktop research in April 2025.

27   "Go-to-Market Fit Toolkit," Oxx, 2023, https://www.oxx.vc/go-to-market-fit/.

28   Jim Barksdale, HBR IdeaCast, episode 413, "Marc Andreessen and Jim Barksdale on How to Make Money," Harvard Business Review, July 10, 2014, 2 min., 52 sec., https://hbr.org/podcast/2014/07/marc-andreessen-and-jim-barksdale-on-how-to-make-money.

29   Hermann Simon et al., Hinnoittelun Voima.

30   The assessment is based on desk research of their packaging approach in April 2025. Their actual packaging approach may differ.

31   Dharmesh Shah, "Insightful Study of 386 SaaS Startup Pricing Pages," OnStartups, March 21, 2016, https://www.onstartups.com/learn-by-example-38-saas-startup-pricing-pages-analyzed.

32   Kyle Poyar, "Insights from 100 SaaS Companies: Why It's Time to Rethink Your Packaging Strategy," Openview, published July 27, 2016, https://openviewpartners.com/blog/insights-from-100-saas-companies-why-its-time-to-rethink-your-packaging-strategy/.

33 Hermann Simon et al., *Hinnoittelun Voima* (Alma Insights, 2021).

34 In our projects, we regularly ask the sales team questions such as: "From your perspective, please rate how price-sensitive customers are in the initial purchase (before they have a working installation) versus when they upgrade or buy add-ons (once they have seen how the system works in practice)."

35 *Pricing Playbook* (Viking Growth, 2024).

36 This book aligns some price model names with this book on SaaS pricing: Ulrik Lehrskov-Schmidt, *Pricing Roadmap* (Houndstooth Press, 2023).

37 Spotify webpage, March 2025.

38 nShift webpage, March 2025.

39 Hermann Simon, Mikael Orvomaa, Felix Mörée, Andreas Jonason, *Hinnoittelun voima*, Alma Insights, 2021.

40 Hermann Simon et al., *Hinnoittelun Voima*.

41 Hermann Simon et al., *Hinnoittelun Voima*.

42 *2024 KeyBanc Capital Markets & Sapphire Ventures SaaS Survey*, (KeyBanc Capital Markets and Sapphire Ventures, 2024), https://info.sapphireventures. com/2024-keybanc-capital-markets-and-sapphire-ventures-saas-survey.

43 *2022 KeyBanc SaaS Survey Results*, (KeyBanc, 2022), https://www.key.com/content/dam/kco/ documents/businesses___institutions/2022_kbcm_saas_survey_10-20-22_vF.pdf.

44 Sometimes, the formulation for a percentage price increase is similar to "[...] any such pricing increase will not exceed X% [...]" to allow for some negotiations.

45 Hermann Simon et al., *Besegra Inflationen*, (Kunskapshuset Förlag, 2023).

46 Kyle Poyar, "From Selling Access to Selling Work (And What It Means for You)," *Growth Unhinged*, October 30, 2024, https://www.growthunhinged.com/p/from-selling-access-to-selling-work.

47 Peter van Westendorp, *NSS-Price Sensitivity Meter (PSM)—A New Approach to Study Consumer Perception of Price*, presented at the 29th ESOMAR Congress in Venice, 1976.

48 André Gabor and Clive William John Granger, "Price Sensitivity of the Consumer," *Journal of Advertising Research*, no. 4 (1964): 40–44.

49 Tim Stobierski, "What Is Conjoint Analysis & How Can You Use It?," *Harvard Business School Online's Business Insights Blog*, December 18, 2020, https://online.hbs.edu/blog/post/what-is-conjoint-analysis.

50 Kyle Poyar, "How to Have "The Talk" with Your Customers," *Growth Unhinged*, January 17, 2024, https:// www.growthunhinged.com/p/your-guide-to-finally-talking-to.

51 Robert B. Miller et al., *The New Strategic Selling: The Unique Sales System Proven Successful by the World's Best Companies* (Grand Central Publishing, 2005).

52 Stanislav Boiko, "How to Optimize Your SaaS Pricing Page—Complete Guide," Cieden, last updated April 24, 2025, https://cieden.com/how-to-optimize-your-saas-pricing-page-in-2022-complete-guide.

53 Read more in: Dan Ariely, *Predictably Irrational: The Hidden Forces that Shape our Decisions* (Harper Perennial, 2010); Enrico Trevisan, *The Irrational Consumer: Applying Behavioural Economics to Your Business Strategy* (Routledge, 2013).

54 Hermann Simon et al., *Ta Betalt!: Hur Pris Påverkar Allt* (Mondial, 2019).

55   Hermann Simon, *Confessions of the Pricing Man: How Price Affects Everything* (Springer, 2015).

56   *ProfitWell Report*, season 4, episode 4, "Which Tactics Will Increase Willingness to Pay?," Paddle Studios, July 9, 2019, https://www.paddle.com/studios/shows/profitwell-report/increase-willingness to pay.

57   Read more about CPQ solutions on Vloxq's website: https://www.vloxq.com/en/resources/what-is-a-cpq.

58   Joseph Schumpeter, *Theory of Economic Development* (Taylor & Francis Ltd, 2021).

59   Andreas Jonason, "Innovative Pricing," (diss., Royal Institute of Technology (KTH), Department of Industrial Economics and Management, 2001).

60   Some examples: Lauren Aratani, "Netflix Tests Charges for Sharing Passwords Between Households," *The Guardian*, March 17, 2022; Jason Murdock, "What Is Netflix Ultra? Streaming Giant Tests More Expensive Subscription Tier," *Newsweek*, July 04, 2018.

61   Kelsey Miller, "5 Critical Steps in the Change Management Process," *Harvard Business School Online's Business Insights Blog*, March 19, 2020, https://online.hbs.edu/blog/post/change-management-process.

62   "Global Pricing Study," Simon-Kucher, 2012.

63   BPP can be made more precise by using the HaaS asset's fully-loaded cost of goods sold (COGS) instead of just bill of materials.

64   "The State of Hardware-as-a-Service," (Silicon Valley Bank, 2024,) https://www.svb.com/globalassets/state-of-haas.pdf.

65   Zachary Kimball, "Developing Hardware-as-a-Service (HaaS) Pricing Plans," *Hardfin*, October 31, 2023, https://blog.hardfin.com/developing-hardware-as-a-service-haas-pricing-plans.

.

www.ingramcontent.com/pod-product-compliance
Lightning Source LLC
Chambersburg PA
CBHW030527210326
41597CB00013B/1053